FIGHTING ON THE BEACHES

A Year of Capoeira in Brazil

By Neil Gleadall

All rights reserved by the author. No part of this publication can be reproduced, stored in a retrieval system, or transmitted in any form, or by any means, without the prior permission of the author.

Copyright © 2006 by Neil Gleadall
All rights reserved.

ISBN-13: 978-1-84728-110-4

ISBN-10: 1-84728-110-9

Acknowledgements

I began writing this book as a diary of events for my friends and family, as I had no idea of how to express my experiences in simple conversation. There was always too much to tell. However, I thank all those who have aided the manuscript in any way, in order for it to become not just an account of my time, but also of some use to others who have embraced Capoeira outside of Brazil.

As Capoeira continues to spread around the world, many more people are fortunate enough to be able to learn such a magical art. It is inevitable that many will be led to Brazil to further their understanding and experience. It is an enormous country of which so many things can be learnt, and would take far more than a year to appreciate even half of them. However, this is the account of my first journey, where I attempted to be as non-judgmental as possible, and to take as much in as I could. I have included all the Mestres and teachers who impacted my journey, and for ease of readability, I have called all Mestres by this respecting title only once, though obviously they are Mestres forever.

Knowing little about how my situation would unfold I was highly reliant on Mestre Gato, his wife Beatrice and their family. I will therefore forever be grateful for their love, friendship and support that gave me such a memorable year. It was only through them that the door opened for me onto a beautiful, eye-opening country, and onto a world of Capoeira, which has helped mould me into a better individual. Their openness allowed me to meet some extraordinary people, whilst never feeling an alien in what to me, was a country unlike I had ever seen before. I will be forever grateful to you all.

I would also like to thank Mestre Peixinho, Mestre Ramos and Mestre Toni, as well as the other teachers of Group Senzala in Rio de Janiero, and also their hard working students. You have provided me with enough teachings, memories and inspiration for a lifetime, and your love for Capoeira will always stay with me.

I was also lucky enough to train with many other Mestres and a special thanks needs to go to Mestre Suassuna, Mestre Acordeon, Mestre Espirro Mirim and Mestre Paulinho Sabia who all touched my Capoeira in their own individual ways.

When I first arrived in Brazil in 2001 I was very much an open book, with many blank pages. This is the story of how some of them were filled. There are an infinite number of ways to enjoy a Capoeira journey in Brazil. I hope you enjoy this one.

Neil Gleadall
25 January 2006

Chapter One

Quem nunca viu, venha ve…
(Who never saw, come see…Popular)

"Can you believe that there are still seven and half hours to go!" said Lee, for the fifth time, although last time he had said it there was seven hours forty-five minutes. I thanked my lucky stars that we were only going to Brazil, and not somewhere further, as I laid back and appreciated the extra legroom that Lee, being six feet, had requested. I, being only five feet five, felt a little cheeky, but not so embarrassed to offer my seat to someone with legs larger than my frog-like pair. I took out my Portuguese dictionary and started reading again, hoping that some of the words might just filter into my brain, and then find a way into my speech. The group of Brazilians, who seemed to find us highly amusing, just highlighted my need to pick up some of the language. Lee had a different itinerary, and as he was only staying for five weeks, as opposed to my year, had little interest in the language, but plenty in the women. To distract me, he showed me the in-flight magazine, which had an interview with Thandie Newton, a more beautiful woman it must be hard to find. As I started reading, Lee piped up again, "Can you believe there's still seven hours left, man this is the slowest journey ever!" Lee was especially good with over dramatizing everything, which I found a little worrying, as he was about to start work as a lawyer when he returned. I had visions of people falling down holes and suing the council, but then Lee turning it into a scene from Tremors, and winning them enormous damages.

Lee and I had met in Capoeira classes in Harlow, Essex. Being of the same age, 22, and of similar levels in Capoeira, we quickly paired up for exercises within class, and had started training at night in empty multi-storey car parks. The avoidance of smashed glass on the floor made the training especially challenging and we liked to encourage each other, always giving the other a push when it was needed. We also both had a large desire to improve quickly, even though neither of us was what would be called a natural Capoeirista (someone who practices Capoeira). Watching the videos from Brazil, and the players' extraordinary movements was mesmerising, and from my very first class I knew I wanted to do this thing 'properly'. Train with the best, and see it for real, in its true environment. As much as I loved the sessions in Harlow's local park, and to a lesser extent, Southend's Multi

Storey, the image I had of doing Capoeira on Copacabana beach was too strong to ignore. The whole package had sold itself to me. Therefore I had bitten the bullet, and quit my job in the City of London. Lee had some spare time on his hands before beginning his job, so Rio beckoned.

I think Lee had been somewhat inspired by another friend, Steve, who had spent two months training with Mestre Gato (Master Cat), and had improved with great leaps. However, apart from his experience we had very little to go on, so ours was very much a great leap into the unknown. We were to stay with Mestre Gato too, and train mainly with the teachers of Group Senzala in Rio. Our teacher in England, Professor Sangue Bom (Good blood), had spent some time with Gato too, and spoke with great awe of the Capoeira in Rio. However, all we knew was that Senzala was a highly respected and established group, with some legendary Mestres, and some damn good students. How would we be accepted? Would the Brazilians mind some foreigners, who weren't even any good, coming to their classes? Was Rio really as dangerous as the books said? How long would it be before Gato would realize how bad my Martello was? Would Lee ever shut up? All these questions were making my head spin, as we crossed the Atlantic.

Gato's house was every bit as impressive as we had been told in England. He lived up in the hills of Rio, in Santa Teresa, an area known for its historic buildings, cobbled streets, arty residents and surrounding Shantytowns (Favellas). Gato's house included an office area, a spacious lounge and a pool that I was to become very well acquainted with. Gato himself was equally as impressive. Lee and I had met him once before in England, but had only passed a few words (fortunately he speaks good English). In his fifties, Gato cut an impressive figure of about five feet nine, looking tanned, fit and strong. He had been a founding member of Group Senzala in the 1960s, and was what I considered a proper Master. He had enormous experience, in both playing and teaching Capoeira, had seen it all, and thus he became an instant hero for me.

He had also been highly successful in his career outside Capoeira (unusual for a Mestre), having taken his Masters in hydrology in England in 1989. It was here that he had started teaching Capoeira in England, and thus how Lee and I had ended up sitting in his kitchen after twenty hours of traveling. Gato's wife, Beatrice, was also considered a Mestre of Capoeira, even though she had never taken a class in her life. However, thirty years of watching, and photographing Capoeira all over Brazil, had given her an insight that very few have. I was always to respect her opinions.

Gato and Beatrice's good looks had obviously spread to their children and even their beautiful (if slightly mad) dog Zekita. Gabriel was only 16, but had his father's natural strength, and opinions beyond his years (though usually far too many). Paula was 24, and though more shy than Gabriel, had the tan and good looks that people almost expect from Brazilians. Needless to say they had both played Capoeira from an early age, and obviously Lee's ever-curious mind was already wondering how good Gabriel was. Their other son, Pedro, was 26, and teaching Capoeira in Scotland. I was yet to know what an effect his group in Scotland would have on my trip.

Lee and I were sharing a room in the house, and as an opening gesture of goodwill I had decided to give him the double bed. However, we did have to share certain things, including the battle with the mosquitoes. I don't think the mosquitoes that lived with Gato could believe their luck, two pieces of fresh meat at the same time, and they were intent on having their party. No matter how much 'Off' spray one put on, there was always a space left for a lucky mozzie, and after a couple of days, Lee and I were admitting defeat in the opening exchanges. Though we were to have our revenge.

With my obsessive ways getting the better of me, and training not yet started, I managed to persuade Lee to go for a long walk toward the Corcovado, and the statue of Jesus that resides there. We were then to run back. Lee was never a fitness fanatic, and decided to walk back, as I ran on. I had been running regularly back in England and had grown to love the feeling of the heart pumping with every stride, but there I had listened to Madonna or something of that ilk on my

Walkman. This run was different however. As I passed the Favella of Fallet, gunshots began to fill the air. Though Gato had warned me about these, I am not sure anything can really prepare someone for the sound, and the noise of a gun fired in anger. It was certainly different from Madonna, and I hadn't run as fast since a large Collie had chased me in Hockley Woods two months before. I returned home safely, though not in 100% health. It seems that the cobbled streets had taken their toll, and I had strained my knee. I couldn't believe my luck. Training was to start seven am the next day.

The alarm went off, and I hobbled out to the pool with Lee. We began stretching as Gato cleaned the pool, and it was at this point that I began to design a stretching routine that incorporated as many movements done whilst lying down as possible. This way I calculated an extra ninety seconds of sleep could be had. Maybe two minutes if you held the stretch long enough, and all, crucially, without Gato seeing you close your eyes. After all, trying to impress a Mestre of Capoeira was highly natural, and was something that I found leading teachers still doing.

Though my knee still hurt, Gato had told me to come up anyway, as he knew some exercises I could do. As Lee began doing some basic movements, I entered the pool, which felt about minus 20C. Gato passed me a flipper, and then told me to drag the flipper against the water, and then flick it out just before it passes through the top of the water. This he told me would strengthen my knee ligaments, and the muscles surrounding them. My face dropped once when he told me to do eighty on each leg, and then again when I saw him begin to give Lee a lesson. Jealousy was not nearly a strong enough word.

As I continued the rather laborious, but challenging exercises, Lee was given what was to become a regular type of Gato lesson. He started doing some basic Ginga, and Angola movements. The ginga is the most basic and essential Capoeira movement. It helps link all a player's movements together, whilst also allowing him to use his body to fake movements to his opponent, whilst keeping within the rhythm of the music. All Capoeira players have their own ginga which develops over the years of training, and Lee's and mine were nothing short of stiff, lacking in rhythm, and allowing us no chance of faking any movement to any opponent. It was only later that Gato admitted what a job he thought he had, when he first saw me ginga. However, soon Gato had a pad out, and Lee was more than content to kick this in the various ways Gato shouted to him, as was something we had always done in the car park.

This type of 'basics' training was to become a regular feature of the year, and the fact that Gato joined in as enthusiastically as he did proved not only his love of Capoeira, but also of the importance of this training. As I had been told before, you can never ginga enough. As for my training, well after about an hour, I was out the pool and lifting weights on my legs, mixed in with sit-ups and pressups, before eating as much as my body would take at breakfast.

As depressing as sitting out the morning training had been, I was more worried about missing the upcoming event. At the weekend, all the Senzala groups would get together to celebrate the beginning of Liga Mundo de Capoeira. This was a new organization, created by Gato, together with several other Mestres, in order for different groups to be in better contact with one another. The event was to include classes by Mestres Gato, Peixinho, Paulinho Sabia and, most excitingly, Suassuna, and I was desperate not to miss it. I quickly threw myself into my pool work, hoping that it would help my knee to heal in time, and on the Friday morning it was time to test it.

Gato had awoken Lee and I every morning of the week at 7am, and now we were feeling it. Lee was shattered, and I think Gato could tell. He made it an easy session, with some basic ginga work, and then more pad work. This was undoubtedly my favourite training, and as long as we weren't doing Martello, I was happy. My kicks were the strongest part of my game, and for a yellow cord, my Armada (an upright spinning kick) and Meu Lua de Compasso (A spinning kick where the body is held lower) were relatively quick. Gato left us to train, and then to look forward to the weekend classes.

Capoeira is best described as a mix between fight, dance and game. This combination takes place in a circle (roda, pronounced 'Hoda') of people, who sing and clap to the rhythms being played by the atabaque (drum), pandeiro (tambourine) and principally, the berimbau. This single stringed instrument leads the roda with various toques (rhythms), and this transmits to the players how they should play. The players use a variety of kicks, sweeps and throws to deceive their opponent, and try to 'catch' him. This could mean, for example, using your ginga to feint to go in one direction, and then kicking in the other, surprising your opponent.

Different toques relate to different styles of game. An Angola game is generally played with low movements, close to the floor, with each player continuously breaking their ginga in an attempt to trick his opponent. The players will also tend to vary the pace of the movements, playing very slowly, and then maybe using a very fast movement to catch their opponent off guard. This is all done to the rhythm being played.

A Regional (pronounced 'Hair-jean-al') style game demonstrates more fight, with the players using higher movements, with more continuous ginga. These games are generally played faster then Angola games, with less expressional movement. However, both games include the dangerous sweeps and throws that can catch any player when he lets his guard down.

Though there is much debate over whether Capoeira was created in Africa and transported to Brazil by the slaves, or whether it was created by the slaves in Brazil, there is no doubting that modern Capoeira was created in Salvador in the early years of the 1900s. Though it was illegally practiced throughout Brazil, Salvador's African roots caused it to grow underground more here than in other cities of Brazil, and gave rise to the Mestres of Capoeira, who are now considered the modern games creators. Mestre Pastinha practiced Capoeira Angola, and by opening his academy in Salvador in 1941, helped the development of Capoeira Angola. Though he died in 1981 many of his songs are still sung in the rodas today, and his students are still held with great respect.

Capoeira Regional was developed by Mestre Bimba, who brought a more formal approach to training, creating sequences that are still used today, and it was his academy that was officially recognized in 1937, that meant the long term ban on Capoeira was finally lifted. He also added many techniques to Capoeira, and though he died in 1974, he is largely seen as the most influential character in its history.

Elsewhere in Brazil, Capoeira developed on the streets, particularly in the North Eastern city of Recife, and in Rio de Janeiro. Thieves and gangs, who were known to also use razors, commonly used it and it was this criminal association that Mestre Bimba managed to break, by moving it into an academy, and more into what is seen as Capoeira today.

Though the weekend event was to begin with Gato's class on the Friday night, it was also to incorporate two seminars to be given by Mestres Itapoan, and Decanio. They were both former students of Mestre Bimba, and thus held in great respect. Lee and I therefore thought we were highly fortunate to be staying in the same house as these great Mestres. They were very different characters however. Mestre Decanio was a very quiet and frail old man, where as Itapoan was stronger and louder character who put Gabriel's opinionated manner to shame. He had an opinion on everything, and was certainly not afraid to voice it. Lee and I were desperate to understand what he was saying, but had to rely on the snippets of interpretation from Gato. One particularly lively discussion had apparently been about the rights and wrongs of Microsoft. So much for my and Lee's assumption of talk of good times and old rodas.

Gato's lesson incorporated some classic 'Gato' movements. We started by practicing passing underneath a Meu Lua de Compasso (a spinning kick where the body is held low) before counter attacking with another one. We then did the basic movement of an armada (an upright spinning kick), countered by a rasteira do chao (a sweep from the floor). By doing an armada, a Capoeira player becomes very open to being swept and Gato trained this sequence often in his classes. However, the danger is that when training it, the person doing the armada prepares his body for a sweep, and falls voluntarily. The first few times of doing this sequence are therefore the most important, as the person doesn't prepare their body. When doing a rasteira, the timing is crucial. If a player can time it correctly, then little force needs to be applied in order to make your opponent fall. I was yet to time one perfectly in two years of training, until now. Lee came crashing to the floor, and was as surprised as me. He soon had Gato shouting at him to land in Negativa, a movement generally used when falling, and me laughing at him. My ankles then got beaten as Lee tried to take me down as I had him.

    The class ended as these things always do, with a roda. The energy that is created by the people involved can be hypnotic, mixed in with the drums and tambourine, and allows the players to feel the rhythm of the music. This was my and Lee's first big roda in Brazil, and we felt very self-conscious. We both lacked the guts to play, as the Brazilians movements intimidated us, and though we knew we would both regret it, we also knew that there would be many more opportunities. After all, this is why we had come to Brazil in the first place. Watching the Roda, Lee and I realized that the Brazilians were every bit as good as we thought they would be. The kicks were fast and direct, with much more fight than in England. Capoeira is still relatively new in England, and thus the lack of experienced players means games are generally at a low level, with a low level of intensity. This was different though. Capoeira in Rio is known for being hard, and the line between game and fight that makes Capoeira such a joyful, but unpredictable experience was much thinner here. One or two games were even broken up as they became too intense, but this was obviously quite normal.

The next day of the celebration saw Mestre Suassuna call off sick, but the arrival of Mestre Paulinho Sabia of Group Capoeira Brasil. He taught in nearby Niteroi, and bought many students with him. He gave a class incorporating the movement of tesoura within different sequences. This movement involves felling your opponent, by locking your own legs round your opponent's body or leg (or arm I was later to learn), and twisting your own body. However, it is a particularly dangerous movement to train, as the sudden twist can easily injure a person, as I quickly found out. My Brazilian partner seemed intent on training the movement with a solid amount of power, and my knee soon strained again under the weight. I couldn't believe it, and ran straight out of the lesson to find some ice. Another week in the pool was not an enticing prospect, so I watched on as Gato encouraged an embarrassed Lee to take part in the African dance of

Makulele, and Lee's Englishness get the better of him as he chickened out.

Lee again avoided playing in the rodas, though I couldn't blame him, as some games got decidedly rough, especially when a student of Paulinho Sabia, Curumim, started to play. He played an aggressive game, using many direct kicks and trying to intimidate his opponent. The better players from Senzala started to see a challenge and were soon buying games with him at every opportunity. The term buying a game is used in Capoeira when a player decides to cut in on someone's game and begin his own game with one of the players.

Curumim was proving very popular, and Lee and I watched closely as one or two kicks started to connect. Though hands were always shaken at the end of each game and it was never violent, the two new students of Rio Capoeira were markedly intimidated.

Chapter Two

E Senzala Senzala, e uma voz que nao se cala
(It's Senzala, a voice you can't shut up – Mestre Toni)

If the recent Liga Mundo da Capoeira event had shown Senzala's strength in Capoeira, Mestre Peixinho's classes showed the reason for that strength. Peixinho (Little Fish) was another founding member of Senzala and was seen as a legend within Capoeira. His Capoeira game contained all the efficiencies that came from his years of training, and the quality of his students spoke volumes for his teaching.

It soon became clear that it wasn't just inside of Capoeira that Peixinho was the epitome of cool. He would spend much of his days on Ipanema beach, where he would arrive on an impressive motorbike, before playing raquette (a bat and ball game Brazilians have taken to a new level) with his friends, and adding to his impressive tan in the sun. He would then take his car, and drive like Michael Schumacher to training, and direct his highly obedient and respectful class. He was obviously immensely proud of his ponytail, and huge sixpack that defied his fifty odd years, and had an aura so intimidating and powerful as I had never felt before. Just by sitting next to him you felt honoured, and getting any advice would feel like striking gold, and this was with good reason. Peixinho took the technical aspect of Capoeira to new levels, and by correcting your feet by as little as six inches he could make large differences to your technique. He would then play one of his expertly self-made berimbaus, and direct his roda with the assurance and confidence of someone who had been doing this all his life, which of course, he had.

Peixinho's current student body certainly included some characters. There was Azeite (Oil) who looked 30, but was actually in his 50s, and no longer played in the roda, but sang each time like it was his first. Cutia, Salaminho, Dolar and Nicholas were regulars at the class, and all under 23. They all played differently with Cutia being small, flexible and with lots of tricks, Salaminho and his one eye being slower, but more powerful. Nicholas was the strongest 15 year old I had ever seen, and was growing more under Azeite's close eye, whilst Dolar, though reaching the grey cord of instructor, showing more enthusiasm than true talent.

Another of Mestre Bimba's legacies was the system of graduation, and this was shown through coloured cords. Senzala's system was as follows:

- White

- Yellow
- Orange
- Grey (Instructor)
- Blue (Formado- graduated student)
- Green (Professor)
- Purple (Professor)
- Brown (Contra-Mestre)
- Red (Mestre)

Each lesson was also usually graced with several green and purple cords, who had been training with Peixinho for several years. Whether it was Koite, Chiquinho, Pedigree or Ninho, all had a level of Capoeira rarely seen outside Brazil, and it was always exciting when you knelt at the berimbau and looked across to see them.

    Fortunately for Lee and I, Peixinho's lessons also included several white and yellow cords, who like us, had been practicing Capoeira for less than two years. We usually stayed at the far end of the class, at the back with these. After a warm-up, Peixinho's classes normally took the same format. Sitting at the front, in his pristine whites, Peixinho would shout an order of movements to a leading student, who then had to show the sequence to the class without being berated by his colleagues. Once he had it correct, Peixinho would then play berimbau and call for the class to do the sequence about eight times, but usually very quickly. He would then stop as everyone panted in an attempt to catch their breath, wait two minutes and start the process again.

After about thirty minutes, the class would then do some sequences in pairs, get tired, start to chat and then have a roda. A roda at Peixinho's would usually consist of two toques (rhythms on the berimbau). The first was Sao Bento Grande de Angola, which was generally played fast, and the second being Jogo de Dentro, which is a game played low, continuous and with little ginga.

At first Lee and I found it difficult to adapt to Peixinho's way. If you didn't pick up the sequence quickly, then there was little chance of picking it up during the class, and thus many of our initial lessons were spent looking at more experienced students, some of whom could look equally confused at times. However, after some time, the sequences began to come and Peixinho's lessons became a joy to take part in. Lee and I would work together, and then try to mix who we played in the roda. Some players were more aggressive than others, and if you were really lucky, then you may get a game with a professor who would come down to your level and let you play.

This is when we would really learn to do which kick when, to esquiva (dodge) in the correct ways, and also when not to do certain things. Lee and I were having similar problems with our games. Our lack of rhythm was obvious, as was our desire to go as fast as possible all the time, and all this whilst not feeling the balance of our kicks. We had a lot to work on, but I seemed to have one distinct problem. I noticed that each time I used the floor, I was caught by my opponent, often by him simply blocking my return. I started to watch the Brazilians play, and saw the grace of movement that Koite had when he went to the floor. He would be up and down as smooth as a yoyo, whilst varying his distance from his opponent to launch his next attack. I began to think of morning training, and how floor work would be imperative.

Though I had only been in Rio for a matter of weeks it was already clear that I was quickly becoming enchanted by the city. The atmosphere in Santa Teresa was that of a small village with a small friendly community. All in it were accustomed to hearing gunshots from the nearby Favellas at night and Lee and I accepted this reality quickly. The first gunshot I heard was whilst I has having a conversation with Gato about the weather. He continued chatting about how hot it could become in summertime despite the nearby shotgun blasts. This was slightly surreal for me, but it was obvious just how accustomed Gato was. I am not sure he even registered the shots.

One night in just our second week, Lee and I were having a drink in a local bar when an enormous blast went off in the same street as we were sitting. Our eyes showed our astonishment and almost panic as we stared at each other.

Before we started running however, we realised it was simply a van backfiring. No one in the bar had moved a muscle and we both felt slightly embarrassed at our 'gringo' reaction. I was to learn with time however.

Another danger with which we quickly became accustomed was of Rio's transport system. Buses ran regularly and Santa Teresa was fortunate enough to also have a century old tram system, which ran into the next district of Lapa. From here we would catch a bus through to training at Copacabana. Though the buses were regular, they also appeared to want to be the fastest mode of transport too. Each driver was a wannabe Ayrton Senna, and when this was added to the thousands of taxi drivers who also thought they were related to the former Brazilian hero, it could lead to some exciting journeys with each driver attempting to weave his way to his destination.

The buses were generally at least twenty years old, which meant only the passengers on board absorbed any bumps in the road, and any speed over 50mph felt like a possible last journey. Lee and I would often sit on the back seat and loved to fly in the air as our bus picked up speed as it descended the viaduct that entered the road along Botafogo beach. A late night bus would then manage to pick up more speed through the curve that entered Flamengo (this is the road that is pictured on many postcards taken from the statue of Christ, overlooking the beaches and Sugar Loaf Mountain).

I always thought this part challenged the drivers more and was sure they had some chart of their top speed on this part of the road. It was undoubtedly the cheapest and best roller coaster I had ever been on.

However, for someone from such a safe and relatively well-organised country as England, this was hugely charming. There were no timetables, no ignoring of passengers who wanted to get on or off at a point that wasn't a stop, no new buses with flash ticketing systems, no letting of people go at crossroads and certainly no embarrassment at using the car horn. It was simply a case of people having more pressing things to worry about and I loved it.

The tram was a perfect example. It meandered down Santa Teresa's cobbled hills on its old tracks with kids jumping on and off when they wanted (anyone who held on didn't have to pay) and the driver playing tunes on the bell or shouting at passers by. It was how I imagined England in the 1920s, and was an ingredient in creating a community atmosphere in the heart of a huge city.

It felt as if people had similar problems and thus were determined to enjoy themselves in every way possible. It was something I felt was lacking in Europe where anything not working correctly is seen as a cause to moan, and rules are kept at every turn. The fact a school kid could jump on a tram, laugh with the conductor and then begin jumping on and off for fun was hugely refreshing for me. I seem to remember the conductor on my schoolbus mostly shouting "sit down and shut up!"

Even the smaller things that many outsiders find annoying I found novel and an important make-up of the city. Street sellers who sold, it seemed, anything from razors and pens, to cakes and juices would even enter the buses to try and make a sale. They gave life to any journey though, and were another example of what makes Rio so interesting. The constant reminders of poverty on a back drop of such stunning natural beauty, along with the obscenely rich mixed into the old and barely usable was a formula which created constant surprises, great characters and very few dull moments.

As my knee began to heal fully, Lee and I were beginning to be launched into a frenzy of morning training. We began to dread Gato's footsteps as he approached our room to wake us up, desperate for another ten minutes sleep. Lee saying "no more, I'm so tired" began to become a regular wake-up call for me, but we both knew that in half an hour's time we would be enjoying another session. It was these sessions that Gato finally got to see how bad my Martello was. The Martello kick is the classic martial arts kick, which can be delivered with speed and power, and requires opening the hips and kicking, usually to the ribs or head, with the front of the foot. I had been carrying an injury in my hip for some time now, and each time I stretched my hips, the injury got worse.

This meant my hips were as stiff as a board, and as a consequence, I HATED MARTELLO.

I would dread the phrase coming up in a sequence, would hate the anticipation of having another teacher telling me to open my hips, and turn my body, and definitely felt a highly unjustified hatred of anyone that could do it well. Gato actually took my problem quite well, and an unexpected bonus actually did come out of his attempts to help me. In order to show me the kick, Lee became Gato's guinea pig, and I sometimes had to bite my lip as I asked Gato to show me once more, knowing Lee's ribs were about to the feel the force of another kick.

After Gato's lesson in the morning, Lee and I would continue with what we thought we needed to work on. This usually involved more pad work (usually at Gato's insistence), and then I had decided to practice the basic movement of going to the floor in negativa. Negativa is used in Capoeira for many different reasons. For example, it is how a player should fall if he is thrown or swept, and it is also used when making use of the floor to move round, or away from, your opponent. In order to practice this, I would use a chair as my 'opponent' and practice moving in my negativa around it. I would also practice going into negativa, changing it to the other side and coming to my feet again, as I noticed many of Peixinho's students using this to avoid a kick and then counter attack. I had promised myself not to go to the floor in a roda until this improved, and was determined to keep to this. After all, doing this for ten minutes delayed me going into the pool and continuing my now dreaded flipper exercises, which Lee still took great delight in seeing me do.

Though these sessions by the pool were leading to some improvements in both my and Lee's games, Gato thought a change of scenery was needed. He gave us the choice, the beach or the mountains. I wanted the mountains, Lee the beach, but it was decided we would do the beach the next day, and the mountains the day after. Beach training has to be taken differently to other training. Though the 2.5 km of Copacabana beach gives ample room for training any Capoeira movement, the sheer unbalancing nature of the sand means some movements are more suited to it than others. As Lee and I cartwheeled around on the sand, Gato decided to take to one of the many fitness posts. We then changed, and started throwing each other, using Vigitiva, a highly powerful technique that when done well can send a player literally flying through the air, as Gato did several times to both Lee and myself. Finally Gato suggested practicing our Bandas, a type of upright sweep, in the sand to help them generate more power, though doing thirty of these on each leg guarantees a good sweat, and a strong desire to run in the sea.

Mountain sessions were very different however, and soon became my favourite morning lessons. With Santa Teresa being high up in the hills anyway, Gato would only need to drive ten minutes to be with Jesus himself, and into Paineras, the surrounding woodland. Beatrice would normally accompany us in order to take in the spectacular views of the city. There was a viewing post that overlooked all of the districts of Lagoa, Ipanema and Jardim Botanico, combining water, the beach and a forest all in one model postcard. This Southern half of the city was the most beautiful and housed many of the richer Cariocas. Though training meant taking your eye off the view, it was these sessions that really brought home where we were. Gato would ask us to do different kicks over the iron fencing, before we could stretch and admire the view once more. I felt in a dream in these sessions, but would soon wake up as Gato asked for twenty Martellos.

Though Lee and I had seen much Capoeira in our short time in Rio, we were yet to go to a Batizado (Baptism), but our chance was soon to arrive. Mestre Bimba had introduced Batizados as a way of graduating his students who had reached certain levels. They had since grown into events that each group would hold, inviting different masters and teachers in order to celebrate with their students. Our first one was to be of an old friend of Gato's, Mestre Touro (Bull), who trained in Penha, Northern Rio. Lee and I arrived in the Brazilian time of one hour late, but soon found a place to watch. We then watched a procession of students receive their new cord, get kicked by several different Masters, before collapsing in exhaustion.

Lee and I were waiting for the real fun to start though. The Batizado had attracted many teachers from all over Rio, and after the graduations they would start to play. However, each student was receiving close treatment, and as always when they are not driving, the Brazilians were in no hurry. It took about three hours before all the graduating students were so exhausted they were wondering whether the new cord was worth it, and the roda begun.

Batizado rodas offer very little chance of a game, unless you are either one, a teacher, two, part of the organizing group, or three, willing to queue for half an hour in the horribly cramped conditions of the instruments, only to be pushed out the game after a few seconds because no-one recognizes you. Lee and I therefore were more than happy to watch especially when the roda soon disintegrated into sheer violence. Like most Rodas, this one started with some nice games, as Peixinho and Touro dictated the sound of the berimbaus. Mestre Beto, a Peixinho student, was clearly enjoying himself, as was Curumim, who I instantly recognized from the Liga Mundo event.

Soon however, the games became quicker, and people were buying into the game just seconds into the game in progress. The buying process was also becoming messy, with people simply jumping in from anywhere to start games, ignoring the usual practice of buying from the berimbau. Tempers were obviously going to flare soon, and when one particular teacher took a Martello to his face, fists began to fly.

Touro soon leapt in (he used to be a freefighter in his younger days), with several other teachers to break the fight, and calm everyone down. The harmony was never likely to last however, and it took only two more minutes before Curumim had wound up one too many people. As he struck out with a fast Meu Lua de Compasso (a spin kick with the upper body low), his opponent entered with an arrastao (a take down involving pulling both legs with the hands). Curumim, however, was aware and countered with a fast Joelho (knee strike), which was met with a big swinging fist (a big swinging fist!) to Curumim's face, and the Capoeira ended again.

It was like being at school again, and I was desperate to shout "FIIIIGGHT" to gather the crowds, but it seemed pointless as most people were actually involved anyway. Soon everyone was separated again, and Curumim's opponent was banished from the Roda. "I hope all the Batizados are like that," said an excited Lee as Peixinho drove us home at an average speed of 100mph through the driving rain.

Chapter Three

E legal, e legal, jogar Capoeira e tocar Berimbau
(It's cool, it's cool to play Capoeira and Berimbau- Popular)

Though Gato's youngest son, Gabriel, was only 16 years old, he looked, and sometimes acted, many years older. The mix of maturity and child appealed to my sense of humour, though sarcasm was often a bridge too far for even the most fluent Brazilian speakers of English, and this was to be the case with Gabriel. We would argue like children before having a political discussion when anything might be the subject.

He tended to pick things up quickly, and when he put his mind to something, he had quite a record of achievement, both at school, and outside. For example, he had only been playing guitar for two years, but was already making live appearances such was his talent. He was also never one to let an opportunity to make money slip away, and it was with this in mind that he offered me some lessons in Portuguese for the princely sum of 10 Reais/hour ($4).

Brazilian Portuguese differs considerably from the language of Portugal mainly due to the pronunciation. Where the Portuguese stress the words more like a Spaniard, a Brazilian flows with informal phrases and slang. Though I was reading books on the subject, I had had very limited practice and thus it was completely alien to me. I had no knowledge of any language other than English and thus a huge challenge awaited me. Like many Latin based languages, once Portuguese is learnt the others can easily follow, but I was starting at virtually zero, as English is not the best basis to have.

The classes would always begin with pronunciation practice, which involved me reading a book, and then Gabriel calling me stupid, when I got a word wrong. Our first lesson lasted one and half hours, where we managed four lines between childish arguments. The second lesson consisted of much the same thing, before I insisted on my 'teacher' preparing for lessons in advance. Gabriel's mature answer was that this was "boring", and so the lessons continued with my pronunciation improving at a snail's pace. This was to continue for some time before Gabriel was 'sacked' for sheer laziness and incompetence. His response was to pick up his guitar and practice again, though we weren't quite finished with the lessons yet.

Where more success was being had, was with the continuing battles with the mosquitoes. Lee had devised a plan to simply blow them away with the power of the ceiling fan, and though this had reduced our bites per night ratio, some were still getting through, despite our covering ourselves with 'Off' spray. We soon found out why. As Lee went to the bin one night, there they were, tens of mosquitoes hiding from the fan under the desk, ready for a night assault. Ten minutes of flip flop pounding later, and we felt confident to get some sleep. The morning sunshine showed two bodies without any new bites.

Unfortunately for Lee, this revenge came just as he had to return back to England, and begin his life as a lawyer. He was clearly proud of his newly acquired muscle and tan, and Gato laughed as he caught him continuously looking in the mirror. We had trained hard together, and I think we both knew that the pain of morning training every day was better shared. However, I couldn't think of a more extreme change in lifestyle, but I had more of a feeling of great sympathy with whoever sat next to him on the plane that afternoon.

Training was continuing well, with my kicks and movements becoming quicker and more balanced, even after just a short time in Brazil. I had always been open-minded about how my training would go. If I calculated it mathematically, I was doing an average of twelve sessions a week. A professor would need about three lessons a week, for ten years to get to such a level, so that was about fifteen hundred lessons. If I continued at my current level of training, then in a year I would have done over six hundred lessons, plus the ones I did in England, and therefore be half as good as a professor.

Fortunately, Capoeira, like any sport doesn't work like maths. The body needs time to learn new movements, adapt to new ways of moving, and though some bodies learn things quicker than others, there is only so quick it can do this. The game of Capoeira is also more than about just movements. I had always been taught that a game of Capoeira is about questions and answers. One player asks a question, for example a Martello, and the other player has to respond in an appropriate way, for example a sweep or a dodge. It is only through training that this response becomes honed to what you want, and this understanding in the mind takes time to learn, and hence the reason it takes so long to be a Mestre of Capoeira. Again, being involved with Capoeira everyday speeds up the understanding of the game, but, at the risk of sounding like George Harrison, it just takes patience and time (and plenty of training of course).

There was one attribute I did want to add to my Capoeira game however, and that was speed. Having seen a collection of teachers in Europe at a meeting in Amsterdam, I had seen how quickly they could react and respond in a game.

It was sensational to watch, and the type of game I most enjoyed. As Peixinho and Gato showed me how to link movements together, and I learnt how to react in a game by playing in the rodas each day, my morning training became focused on trying to do my movements with balance, and speed. Kicking a pad as fast as possible was not only making me physically fit, but also helping me generate more power in each kick. It was also highly enjoyable, and made me want to play in the rodas as much as possible, and compare to how my game was improving with others at my level. Peixinho's next class gave me that chance.

Usually Peixinho gave classes to about twenty people at a time. However, on this particularly humid night (I was currently drinking about three to four litres of water per class), there was about twice that number of students. A teacher from the state of Minas Gerais had brought along his students, and the roda was larger than normal, but also at a lower level. I decided to play as much as possible, until my third game. Though still playing with a lack of rhythm, my floor movements had improved enough to start using the floor again in games, though I was still consciously restricting it. Another yellow cord cut in my game and straightaway, he attempted to catch me with a rasteira. His attempts were rather unsubtle though, and as I gave a bencâo (a straight push kick), he tried a banda (an upright sweep). However, instead of sweeping my leg, he simply hacked my shin. Peixinho stopped the roda and told him this was unacceptable. The game finished soon after and I expected a big bruise the next day.

It was also at this time that I started training with another Senzala Mestre, Toni Vargas. Mestre Toni was another student of Peixinho, and was famous within Capoeira for his music. He had appeared on, and released many CDs of Capoeira music, and his voice could give a roda energy like no other. Though a big intimidating man of over six feet, he was infinitely welcoming and he was never scared to let his emotions out, often dedicating his songs to certain people. His style of teaching was very different to that of Peixinho's. His warm-ups were always entertaining, often using the drum rhythm of Makulele, and, perhaps allowing for less experienced students than Peixinho, his sequences shorter. His roda also contained a different energy, opening with the rhythm of Angola, and then building the energy until it reached a crescendo in the very fast regional games. I always made sure I saved some energy for these games.

Toni's group also reflected his outgoing, friendly character. Going to his classes was never as intimidating as being at Peixinho's, with people always willing to share a joke amongst the whole group. Doboru was a blue cord who had been training with Toni for six years, and liked to practice her English with us. Lobo (Wolf) was a green cord, and Toni's most senior student. Though he often played an aggressive game, his Capoeira was expressive, quick and strong, and he was the sort of player that you could learn from just by watching him. Caculee was a student who had come to Rio from Minas Gerais just to train with Toni, and was improving at a rate of knots, and was to gain his blue cord after some time. Samurai and Geisha were a brother and sister, who played similar Capoeira, as well as both being architects. Their command of English was good, and even though they were reasonably new to Toni's group, and Capoeira, their friendship helped me settle into the group's sessions.

It was in one of these faster Rodas at Toni's that I got to play Contra-Mestre Jacare (Alligator). He had taken the class as Toni was unwell, and the roda had good energy with Professor Chao (Floor) visiting from France. I had just played Chao in what was a good game, and was feeling the most confident I had felt in my time in Brazil, when Jacare bought my game. I had seen Jacare play in a roda at Peixinho's class and knew he could play very fast as times, but with control in his kicks. He, like Chão, was playing at my level however, and we were enjoying the exchange of feints and kicks. I then went to do an Armada and he came towards me to sweep my leg. I managed to avoid being taken down, but at quite a cost. Jacare caught me directly on my recently required bruise, and I ended the game shortly afterward. At the end of the class, Chão paid me a compliment in telling me how well I had played. I thanked him before hobbling off, cursing Jacare, and holding my left leg.

With my head swelling after Chao's compliment, I threw myself into more training, knowing that it was beginning to pay dividends. The weekend coming was time for another batizado, this time of Mestre Paulinho Sabia, just across the Guanabara Bay in Niteroi. As Paulinho was a founding member of Capoeira Brasil, and a former member of Senzala, I was expecting the event to be large, and I wasn't disappointed. Mestre Boneco, another founding member, had flown in from Los Angelas, and joined a host of other teachers and Masters. The Capoeira was very quick paced, and the large crowd ensured that many of the players showed off their acrobatics.

As Capoeira players develop great skills in flexibility and body control, acrobatics can come relatively easy to some players. Hence, they are appearing more and more in Capoeira, especially with the increase in demonstrations around the world. There are now even some groups that specialize in these movements, but this can take away from the game. Capoeira is a two-person game, but by doing too many acrobatics, the game can be lost. I played with many people throughout my time in Brazil, and sometimes was unlucky enough to play someone who concentrated more on flipping around than exchanging "questions and answers" with me. I can't think of a more boring game of Capoeira, than a one-player game.

Paulinho's batizado gave a whole section devoted to Mortals (somersaults), and the crowd responded highly enthusiastically. As the players became more encouraged, more daring Mortals were done, until the inevitable crash happened. A professor tried a flip too expansive and he came crashing down on a member of the watching audience. I am not sure what was more hurt, his back or his ego. The most impressive Professor however, was Tourneiro, who looked the complete athlete. His dreadlocks, six pack stomach and delicacy of movement stood out even in this high level company. I was later to learn that he was actually a Senzala student from Teresopolis, and though he now taught in Paris, had learnt under the teaching of Mestre Elias. How good could Capoeira get? I thought, as we traveled back over the 13km bridge to Rio.

It was also at this event that I met Brie, a tiny Canadian girl, who had recently spent some time in Scotland, where she had been training with Gato's eldest son, Pedro. She was highly excited to meet Gato and Beatrice again, and though she was supposed to be going to Porto Alegre in the south of the country to do charity work with street kids, she couldn't stop talking about training and when we were going to start. Her cute features, and hugely friendly manner, had left quite a mark with Gato and Beatrice when they had visited Scotland,

and she was due to move into the house the next week. I was pleased to have found a new partner after Lee's departure, and we talked Capoeira all afternoon, in anticipation of morning training the next week.

Morning training took on new significance as Brie and a further member of Pedro's group, Panda, joined me. I was never to find out Panda's real name, as in Capoeira nicknames stick. Nicknames in Brazil are commonplace, with people receiving them for numerous reasons, but hold a particular relevance in Capoeira. When it was banned in the early part of the 1900s, Capoeiristas, when caught, were often interrogated by the police before being whipped. To avoid giving away their comrades, the idea of nicknames was started, and has remained a tradition ever since. Brie was known as Formiguinha Atomica (Atomic Little Ant), which always raised a smile amongst the Mestres, for her small frame, but highly energetic way.

She was, in fact, a bundle of energy. A strong North American accent was ever prominent, especially when everything was always described with the word 'totally' coming before each adjective. Capoeira was "totally" cool. Brazil was "totally" hot. Gato's house was "totally" awesome. Though it was sometimes like having a soundtrack to an American sitcom playing, Brie's charm more than overcame it. She was instantly likeable, and was to make a big impression on the many people she met.

After being a child dancer, Brie had come across Capoeira in Canada before travelling to Scotland. Her love for it was obvious, and immediately I sensed her plans to go to Porto Alegre were subject to change, as proved the case.

Panda was known as such because of his small, but somewhat rotund frame. Though he was smaller in height than me, Panda was big in bulk, and earned his money being a bouncer on the doors of Dundee. He also claimed to be highly experienced in martial arts, learning various forms over twenty years. Gato later questioned this, as Panda was only 26 years old, and as we later found out, prone to exaggeration, and sometimes outright lying.

To welcome the new members, Gato decided to set an example at the pool and stay for the whole session. Panda had a problem with his knee, so Brie and myself had to contend with Gato's insistence of kick after kick on the pad, followed with entrances in Vigitiva (a throw) and Cabeçada (headbutt). Exhausting, especially when in Peixinho's class later, the pads came out again and we did Armada, after Armada. This method of repetition had actually come into common use in Capoeira in the 1960s, when Gato and his fellow Senzala friends found it a great way of perfecting technique. It was used by just about every school I went to in Brazil and though my body was slowly becoming used to this incessant kicking,

Brie's hadn't yet had time to adjust, so I was astounded as she did kick after kick without stopping. I actually drifted away at one stage whilst holding the pad, until I realized she was still going. An atomic ant indeed. Meanwhile, a common trend began, as Panda again sat out the class.

The next day was much the same thing, until my nightmare occurred. I had a feeling that things were going too well, and when Gato started breaking his ginga and moving in ponte (a bridge), I whispered to Brie "this is where I fall over". Whether this was self-fulfilling or not, I had to admire my prediction, as on the second time of trying I went over, and straight onto my knee. The poolside floor was unforgiving, and I knew the moment it happened something was wrong. I decided to sit out the rest of the session, and Gato's class that night to see how it felt in the morning.

Watching Gato's lesson was painful, as I always enjoyed his relatively relaxed, but still challenging classes, but not as painful as the knee the next day. In between watching more lessons, and secretly noting down the sequences taught, I iced the leg and hoped it would be good enough to take part in the workshops that were to form Mestre Elias batizado weekend, in Teresopolis in three days time. Apart from looking like another well supported batizado, the meeting also held an added excitement for me, as Tourneiro would be there. Entertainment guaranteed.

Chapter Four

Eu tenho Axe, eu tenho axe
(I have the energy, I have the energy...Mestre Toni)

Rio can get hot, very hot. Summer temperatures can reach over 40C, and even in winter it can be over 30. Cariocas deal with this heat in various ways. The rich use air conditioning, and round every street corner is a juice bar, all selling a huge variety of fruits, many of which, despite my immense experience as a schoolboy working in the produce section of a supermarket, I had never heard of. Some just give in and lay on the beach soaking up as much sun as they can, though mostly with protection (Brazilians are very conscious of their skin). There is a further way to escape the heat, and that is to head to the mountains.

Teresopolis is a one hour drive from Rio, which is mostly uphill. The winding roads of the mountain mean that driving here was even more perilous than in Rio, with lorries overtaking with ludicrous, pugnacious enthusiasm and regularity. Even so Gato, with his three Gringo students in tow, arrived at his Mother-in-law's house, where we were to stay the night for the batizado event of Mestre Elias. The house was spectacular, with stunning views of the surrounding mountains. In fact, Teresopolis is famous for its views, as well as being the training camp for the Brazilian football team.

We arrived in time for Brie to take part in the women only class. This is something that has begun to appear in Capoeira recently, for whatever reason. Gato explained how he couldn't really see the point, as Capoeira is a game for all, and, with their natural flexibility, women are often equally as good as men, though their entrance into the sport has only really been more recent. To encourage divisions between men and women, where none exist, is something I couldn't fully understand, and there was little difference in the lesson to any other I saw in Brazil.

As I expected, the batizado had attracted many Mestres and teachers, and the evening roda in the Town Square was spectacular. Toni led the energy on the microphone, as Mestres Peixinho and Itamar played the berimbaus. Tourneiro, and a fellow professor, Michel, stole the limelight in the rodas themselves with their sheer speed and technique. Gato also looked to be enjoying himself as he executed a perfect rasteira da chão on an unsuspecting player. In typical Brazilian fashion, everyone then moved to the nearest bar, where the Mestres were given their own table. Also done with typical Brazilian style was Mestre Marinaldo's hitting on Brie. This was to become commonplace at these type of events, as the

Brazilians loved Brie's outgoing way, and her communication with them in Spanish. It was certainly not the last time Brie needed saving.

The next morning Gato provided a saving grace for Brie. By oversleeping, she missed Mestre Itamar's lesson. Itamar was another founding member of Senzala, whose voice and music had accompanied thousands of rodas, but whose receding hairline and ponytail showed his age. His last visit to Scotland had also given him the chance to hit on Brie, and though she appreciated his friendship, she wasn't too upset over missing his lesson.

Despite my best efforts, my knee hadn't healed in time so I was ready for more torturous watching of lessons. Panda was still also complaining of his knee, but had decided to train. We arrived just in time for Peixinho's lesson, which incorporated many movements of Martello in his sequences, and showed them all, using Tourneiro as his guinea pig. My hip and I breathed a sigh of relief as I avoided another Martello session.

The lesson ended with a roda in the local market. Mestre Claudio, an Angoleiro from Bahia, gave the roda added energy as Brie battled to get a game with the "gorgeous Tourneiro", and Panda sat out again complaining about more pain in his knee. He had now been in Brazil for two weeks, and I had seen him play only once. His Capoeira was good considering his short time training with it, and I couldn't understand his increasing reluctance.

The actual batizado wasn't due to start until the early evening, which gave Gato time to take us to some waterfalls within the mountains. Though he had been born in Recife, Gato had spent most of his life living in Rio and thus knew a beautiful spot just outside of town. The backdrop of forest and running water gave a highly tranquil atmosphere, which was soon ruined as Brie and I slid down rocks into the natural springs that, though cold, gave a huge cleansing sensation. Even Panda had a smile on his face, which was beginning to become a rarity.

The batizado itself took place, as they often did, in a five-a-side football court. Crowds of parents eager to see their children receive their new cords, and desks selling Capoeira merchandise surrounded the place. Brie found this merchandise, mainly t-shirts and trousers, nothing short of "totally" irresistible and I became accustomed to having to recommend which child size T-shirt I liked best, or which pair of trousers I preferred. It was here that the theory of Yellow trousers was invented. Brie had noticed that in the market roda, only good Capoeira players wore yellow trousers, including Tourneiro, which, Brie claimed, made them look "totally cool". It was therefore decided that anyone who wore yellow Capoeira trousers either had to be good, or was bringing the game into disrepute. With this being batizado though, all the participants were in their cleanest white uniforms, awaiting their new cords.

Brie and I managed to find a decent viewing spot, whilst Panda wandered off, not to our disappointment, on his own. Toni and Itamar shared the singing, as Mestres Elias, Gato, Boa Gente (from Bahia), Itapoan and Peixinho played the children of the group. This is generally the order of Batizados, with cords given out in order, starting with the lowest. After finishing with the children, the group performed some Makulele. This is an African dance that over a number of years has been intertwined with Capoeira, especially at events and demonstrations. The dance is performed to a beat on the Atabaque, and is often done with sticks or swords clashing together. The group, dressed in traditional African clothes and facepaint, performed the dance under candlelight, and to the sound of Tourneiro's drumbeat. The rhythm can be quite intoxicating, and with the mix of sticks, is nothing short of exhausting when performed at high speed.

The roda was then reformed, as it was the more senior students turn to receive their new cords. For neutrals, this is where batizado events can become boring. In a large group, the receiving of white and yellow cords can take literally hours, and the Capoeira is limited in its intensity. I could sense Brie's eyes beginning to close, when finally the more senior students were given their cords. As each name was read out, the student was 'comically' beaten by his fellow Capoeiristas, and then played until exhaustion by various professors and Mestres. It was after this that the real fun started, as the energy grew and grew. The rhythm became faster, and Toni's voice was being met with enormous enthusiasm from the students, who were all jumping around at the edge of the roda, showing off their new cords. Only Tourneiro and Michel had the speed to play to this rhythm, and their legs became a blur as their kicks and jumps intertwined like I had never seen in a roda before. Curumim continued to buy the game, but didn't have the same pace in his movements, and a Professor who had flown in from Argentina, despite wearing yellow trousers, had the same problem. Michel and Tourneiro, kicked and flipped, whilst the other Capoeiristas sang to Toni's rhythm. I had never seen anything quite as good as this, and Brie and I were wide eyed with our jaws on the floor. As the roda stopped to enormous applause, I soon realized that this is what I meant by the "true environment".

Back in Rio, I was currently sleeping on Gabriel's bedroom floor. He would have his window open, and each night I would listen to the various insects whilst looking at the clear skies. The peace was only interrupted by the odd late night gunshot, or passing police patrol. Occasionally a party would be raging in a local Favella with what I considered to be the largest speakers in the world. I would soon doze off however, knowing that Gabriel would wake me up by deliberately treading on me at 6am, the time he rose for school. I would then doze for an hour.

After being on such a high with the batizado, reality once again hit home as Gato woke us all up for morning training at 7am on Monday. I was able to do some gentle exercises in my ginga as my knee improved, Brie trained as usual, like a girl possessed, and Panda sat and moaned whilst he lifted some weights. Panda's attitude could be quite complexing at times. His moods were almost schizophrenic, altering between the life and soul of a party, and then the like a man who had been shown his deathbed. He would show signs of being homesick by talking of his home in Dundee, and his family. His sombre, skeptic way however, was always going to conflict with Brie's hyper personality, and it didn't take long before I felt stuck in the middle. Bickering became the order of the day, and if I felt there was a chance to separate the two then I would take it. As Panda wasn't training much, it meant that Brie and I spent much more time together going to lessons, and usually partnering up for exercises. I would then try and go for a drink with Panda in the evening, but this usually ended up with him moaning of Brie's ways.

Training was definitely an escape from this tense atmosphere, and still being inspired by Tourneiro's showing at the batizado, Brie and I trained as hard as possible at Peixinho's classes. I finally had the hang of capturing the whole sequence quickly, and thus could keep up with the rest of the class.

We had also started training with another Senzala Mestre, and Peixinho student, Mestre Ramos. Ramos oozed energy, and his enthusiasm for Capoeira was simply overwhelming. Gato once told me how he used to work ten hour days, before coming from the other side of Rio (he is from the district of Ramos, hence the name) to train in the evening, and then do the same the next day. He was also one of the strongest people I had ever met. Though only five feet nine, his body was rippled with muscle, and together with his moustache, gave the impression of an army sergeant. Though he taught his classes in the district of Bangu, he had decided to begin some afternoon lessons in the same academy used by Gato and Peixinho in Leme, and hence killer Tuesdays and Thursdays were born. This meant a 7am session with Gato, a 5pm session with Ramos, followed by a 7:30 session with Gato again. Lifting a leg in Gato's class began to become a struggle, and Brie and I soon noticed that each time Gato saw us play, we were exhausted, and thus played badly. It was that impressing your Mestre conundrum again.

Ramos gave a good class. In fact, some of his lessons were the best I took in Brazil. The small numbers, caused by the class being in the afternoon, meant that you received close attention and your mistakes were spotted quickly. However, when the roda began, the small numbers meant you had to play almost constantly. Playing Capoeira is training in itself. It is by playing that you learn what movements to use and when, as well as learning the interaction involved in a game. This interaction involves the trading of kicks and dodges, but also moving around your opponent and trying to confuse him with a serious of fakes and other movements. It was in this aspect that Ramos' lessons helped enormously. He would usually put on a Mestre Acordeon CD, and just let us enjoy the game, whilst attempting to use the movements we had trained in the class.

We also began taking music lessons with Ramos, and here he excelled again. Music is a crucial part of Capoeira, and there are myths surrounding its inception. Some believe that the slaves introduced the music to Capoeira in order to disguise the fight as a dance, but there is also evidence that suggests the slave owners actually used the Capoeira fighters like fighting cockerels, and thus knew exactly what Capoeira was. Whatever the truth, music is very much part of Capoeira, and are lessons in themselves. Many songs speak about the history of the game, telling about the sailors who used to play in Salvador, or even of mythical slaves who fought for freedom. The berimbau provides the rhythm for the game, and when they are combined with skill, they help provide the adrenaline and energy that players want whilst in a roda.

It was also something I needed to improve on whilst I was with the best. Ramos would sit us down with berimbaus, and start us playing one of the regular toques. He would then introduce a break in the toque and we would practice on his count. Once we had this, a song would be introduced, and we would take turns in taking the lead. This brought together all the important aspects in giving the roda energy, the music, the people and the songs. The majority of beginners in Capoeira are inevitably nervous when confronted with the prospect of singing, but Ramos was not only a Mestre of Capoeira, but proved to be a Mestre of filling people with confidence as we happily repeated the songs he taught us. My nerves would slowly disappear as I would try to sing in my best accent, even if this was still 100% gringo.

There are songs in Capoeira that are popular in all the rodas of the world, and it was these that Ramos initially taught us, gradually moving on to different verses and choruses. The good humour and ever-smiling Mestre certainly helped the music filter in to our memories.

With the imminent arrival of Gato's eldest son, Pedro, from Scotland, as well as more students from the UK, Brie and I thought it best to make some room at Gato's house and move on. Though Mestre Peixinho lived with his family in Ipanema, he also looked after a house, just ten minutes walk from Gato's. As soon as Brie saw the tree that grew in the middle of the lounge and out the roof, along with the wooden balconies that over-looked a sizable house, she had decided she wanted to move in. I agreed more reluctantly, as though the house was close to Gato, and thus morning training, it was also in the Favella of Fallet. Though living at Gato's meant we had overlooked the Favella of Morro do Coroa, and heard the numerous gunshots that left it, moving to Peixinho's house meant we were that much closer to the 'action'.

The steps that ran down from the main road of Santa Teresa, soon to become known as the "Steps of Doom", formed the main entrance to Fallet. Peixinho's house was situated just a hundred yards from the bottom of the steps, which meant we had to walk in the Favella to reach the house, something very few Gringos do, except on organized tours. This left me feeling nervous. Some former residents had told me about seeing men with guns casually walking up the road, and Peixinho's 'rules' didn't help to settle my nerves. He told us to never come if we saw the police, and if we received any trouble to talk with him, not the police. He also told us to wait at least twenty minutes before leaving the house if we heard gunshots. I thought this last rule was perhaps a bit unnecessary to point out.

Rio is famous for its shanty towns and their erratic and hap-hazardous construction has even led to a new form of architecture. I had even studied them as part of a geography course when I was fourteen, and here I was now living in one. Each Favella is 'owned' by members of one of the two major gangs of Rio, Commando Vermelho (Red command) and the Commando Terceiro (Third Command), who run the drugs market associated with it. Fallet was currently owned by Commando Vermelho, which means that it was often attacked by bandidos (bandits) of Commando Terceiro, who attempted to take the territory. It was these shootouts that posed the biggest threat to Brie and I. The Favellas residents knew that we were students of Peixinho and would never threaten us, but getting caught in crossfire was a possibility, whether it be between the gangs, or when the Police arrived to quash any fighting (or perhaps collect any money due!).

It didn't take us long before we began to recognize the differing sounds of the bandits' guns, and those of the Police. If you were 'lucky', another Favella may start using tracer bullets, which lit up the sky with orange traces, much like Star Wars. The majority of nights were quiet, but occasionally a turf war would open up, and each night our sleep would be interrupted with shooting, sometimes directly outside the house. It wasn't uncommon to find empty bullets on the floor outside our gate of a morning.

The most unnerving experience, however, became the steps of doom. Each night after training, the bus would drop Brie and I off at the top of these steps, and each night we would walk down slowly whilst listening for sounds of fighting below. The heart would sometimes start to pound if it had been a bad week.

Despite its inherent dangers, the house did give Brie and I more freedom. We started to cook big meals, full of carbohydrates, whilst drinking energy drinks, and making conversation with Mario. Mario was a man in his eighties, and being an old friend of Peixinho's, looked after the house. His days were simple, sitting out the front of the house, and chatting to the neighbours about the latest gossip (and it was certainly more interesting than the local gossip at home. Who was shooting who…). At night he would sit and watch television in his room. He lived downstairs in the basement, where during the day, the dog, Black was kept. Black was a rottweiler, and a very big one at that. He looked very sick, with large patches of bare skin, where he had a disorder, and was often surrounded by fleas. This unhygienic atmosphere extended to the pool, which hadn't been used, or cleaned, for what seemed like years. It seemed such a waste that such a beautiful house was falling apart, just because of its location.

Pedro helped us move in, and we received many strange looks from the local residents, and even stranger ones from the Bandits, who we found out spent their time at the end of our road. Pedro decided to ask where Peixinho's house was, just to calm their nerves. It wasn't to be the last time we were to see their guns. I took the smaller room for the simple reason that it had a view of Northern Rio, and therefore the Maracanã stadium, where most of the football was played. Not a day went past when I wouldn't look at it and admire its sheer enormity. Reality soon hit home again, though, as Brie and I realized that we had to get up ten minutes earlier for morning training, and walk the hundred and twenty-one steps of doom.

Morning training continued as usual. Brie and I would work hard, Panda would complain about an injury and sit at the side, and Gato would give us several exercises to do before going off to work. Pedro's presence made a pleasant change however, and some mornings he would give us a class. He knew both Panda and Brie well from Scotland, but I had only met him briefly at the Amsterdam event. It soon became obvious that Pedro was in fact just a tall version of his brother, Gabriel. They acted the same, spoke English with the same accents and phrases, and had an equal number of opinions. Several times after training, I would have a debate with Pedro, and if Brie was there, it quickly turned to aggravating her. Something Pedro had a very special talent for.

It was after one of Pedro's lessons that I begun to realize the possible extent of the problems with living in a Favella. I was walking back to Fallet, when I noticed two police cars at the top of the steps of doom. This obviously immediately aroused my suspicions, but it was only when I got closer that I noticed that two of the Police were pointing rifles down the steps and onto, what was now, my road. I stood and watched for a moment, before deciding to invoke

Peixinho's first rule, and come back later. Though I heard no shots this time, as I sat back at Gato's house in my sweaty clothes, I did begin to wonder what I had let myself in for by moving into this house.

Chapter Five

Esse Gunga e meu, a gunga meu foi meu Pai que me deu
(This is my Gunga, my Gunga my father gave me...Popular)

Gato's classes in Brazil were always more relaxed than those of the other Senzala teachers. This doesn't mean we didn't train hard in his lessons, just that there was a more informal atmosphere within the class. Gabriel would spend much of his time trying to distract me, or simply criticizing my Martello, which hadn't improved at all with my training. In fact the opposite had occurred. The sheer intensity of the training was making my hip worse, and thus my Martello had actually got worse in my time in Brazil. This was a particular problem in Gato's lessons, as his sequences often included the movement. I would somehow manage to get by in this part of the class, and hope the next sequence would be different.

The other difference in Gato's lessons to other Senzala Mestres was that he tended to play some Angola in his roda. Senzala is very much a Regional style based group, but does play some Angola at times. It is believed that training in one will help the other, and I found this to be true. Peixinho's rodas would always be played with fast games or the Jogo de Dentro (inside game) that his students were so good at, Ramos also tended to play to a fast rhythm, and though Toni would build his more slowly, the majority of games were Regional. It was nice to have the occasional change that Gato's lessons offered.

Gato's other distinction was his amazing ability to attract more eccentric students. Apparently this had always been the case, and his current student body was no different. Freitas was initially nicknamed The Mule, by Lee and I, as in the roda he would kick and kick, often without purpose. He had been a student of Gato's many years before, and reached a good level, but was now returning after a long break. Nils was another older student of Gato's, who would often corner me after a class to practice his English, but didn't realise, that though pleasant, he was also incredibly boring.

The most eccentric though, was Dolfino. With his crazy haircut of a step an inch above his ears, and large moustache, Dolfino gave the impression of an eccentric, and he didn't disappoint. Each night he would give the most enthusiastic handshake, whilst nodding and continuously saying "Tudo Bom, tudo bom" (everything alright?). He would then move his cap back to front for the lesson, before again shaking your hand and saying "Até quinta, até quinta meu amigo" (until Thursday my friend). Shaking hands at the end of a lesson was a ritual that could take twenty minutes after Peixinho's class, and Toni's students had some impressive variations, but Dolfino's nodding and enthusiasm could almost be unnerving in its ferocity.

Training was continuing well. Brie and I had settled into a routine of lessons, and the coming bank holiday weekend was going to give us an opportunity to see some more Capoeira outside Senzala. This is something I was keen to do, as much as was enjoying Senzala's training. I had been told that Capoeira was different all over Brazil, and different groups trained in different ways. Gato's invitation to Mestre Sena's event in Poços de Caldes, Minais Gerais, was about to give us the chance to see, and train, with some different groups and teachers. Gato decided to hire a large car for the trip, which was just as well, because for the seven hour drive, Panda took the majority of the back seat from Brie and I. Beatrice had also decided to come, but was looking nervous at the prospect of me sharing the driving on the way home.

In usual style we arrived late, and Gato left Panda, Brie and I at the hall being used for intermediate classes, before rushing off to give his own lesson elsewhere. We rushed into the class, which was being taken by a Mestre whom I didn't recognise, and didn't see get introduced, but was obviously already warmed up, as after five stretches, he had us doing macacos. This movement is acrobatic in nature, and I could envision pulling several muscles at once by doing it now, so I moved off to the side to watch the hundred or so students start banging into each other. Panda, who was particularly unhappy, and called the class "a joke" then started telling me that he was thinking of quitting Capoeira. He had been hit quite hard by the recent death of his Grandmother, but I couldn't see his reasoning. I felt for him, especially being away from home at a bad time, but what would quitting Capoeira achieve? Especially when he had traveled half way around the world to train in it. I left him to his thoughts.

Mestre Museu, who was based in Belo Horizonte, took the next lesson. He gave a good class, which was based around countering a Meu Lua de Compasso by entering in tesoura, and falling your opponent. I was still lacking a little confidence when using this move since my earlier knee injury so I was happy to be partnering Brie, as Panda again sat and watched from the side. Museu ended his class with a roda that soon turned farcical. After ten minutes, the queue to play was covering the sight of the berimbaus, and games were being bought after just seconds. I managed to buy one game, only to get hacked on the shin when giving a Quixada, and then be bought out immediately after. Brie had more success managing at least three kicks in her two games.

Gato, who again trained a sequence including tesoura, gave the final lesson of the day. It seemed to be only at these events that we trained this movement. It is very difficult to use it in a roda, as the timing and technique need to be perfect, but also done at high speed, as the entrance needs to be done so your opponent doesn't have time to respond. Gato finished his class with three rodas, something he liked to do when there were many people, and it made sense. The rodas still contained enough energy, and everyone got to play for a reasonable amount of time. Taking out my frustration of my one game in Museu's roda, I played as much as I could, and by the end, was exhausted and ready for a rest.

Being with Gato and Beatrice meant we got to stay with all the Mestres and teachers, at a farm owned by Sena. The guest rooms were basic, but spacious enough, and the large pool looked inviting for the next morning. However, the night was to be taken up with a talk on Capoeira in a local theatre. A large table was placed on a stage for all the Mestres to sit, and then questions from the audience. My Portuguese lessons with Gabriel had prepared me for very little, and thus trying to understand a discussion was out of the question. Whilst we waited for Gato's summary, Brie spent an hour choosing another T-shirt.

Though missing out on the discussion had been annoying, Gato was actually jealous of me. It turned out that Mestre Rêne, an Angoleiro from Salvador, had, in Gato's eyes "ruined it". Whatever the discussion was on, Rêne turned it into a question of Race, and even claimed that Capoeira was being "stolen by the whites". This type of controversy seemed interesting to me, and I was even more disappointed at missing the discussion.

Though the next day's lessons started at 8am, we were now accustomed to Brazilian timing, and Gato didn't disappoint. It seemed that the classic and entertaining game of Poohsticks had somehow missed Canada, so after teaching Brie the rules, seeing her win and having a swim afterwards we arrived for training at 1pm. This meant we arrived just in time for Mestre Burgues' lesson. Burgues was head of Grupo Muzenza, who had many schools in the south of Brazil. It was a Regional group, and Gato had warned me that they liked to play hard. Brie and I took the lesson as Panda watched once again, claiming he had had too much sun. The lesson consisted of some regional based sequences.

The roda was then formed, and Burgues led on the berimbau. He had brought some students with him, and they were huge, imposing figures. Two in particular played a lot, and then I saw what Gato meant. One, Brie and I nicknamed him Meathead, had a particularly fast game, but very little subtlety. We watched as he seemed to try and kick at his opponent at every turn. As his younger, less experienced and smaller opponent raised his hand to end the game, Meathead fired a fast Martello straight into his face. Brie and I weren't the only ones to "ooh" in shock, and the young player was stunned, just standing in the roda in disbelief. Burgues carried on playing the berimbau, as two new players began playing, whilst praying Meathead wouldn't buy a game with them. Panda stormed off in protest but I stayed for the rest of the roda. I didn't consider playing but the incident showed how careful one had to be in the roda. The fight aspect would always be present, and one would always have to be on guard.

Speaking to some of the Brazilians later, it seemed that they were as shocked as Brie, Panda and I had been, but it showed that one should always be aware of their opponent. It was the talk of the class, but just showed how dangerous Capoeira can really be. The movements are strong, and can cause considerable damage, possibly even death if executed fully on someone. One of the things that always attracted me to Capoeira was the thin line between fight and game, knowing that one aggressive movement, or deliberately placed kick can quickly change the nature of the game, gives a fascinating feeling of living on the edge, and a true adrenaline rush. Now I had seen it for real, I was no longer a doubting Thomas.

The day continued with a lesson from Mestre Mao Branca, who is also based in Minais Gerais, and based most of his class around moving in the ginga, something I desperately needed to work on. My ginga was still stiff, and with little expression. Each roda I watched, I was noticing more and more, how much a player could use his ginga. With a good amount of subtlety in his ginga, a player could trick, feint and move around his opponent with ease, and I had none of this. I was determined to memorise Mao Branca's class, and use it in my morning sessions, and this I did, until he too decided to train some movements in Tesoura. I had never done so many Tesouras in my life.

Our final lesson of the weekend was to be taken by Mestre Rêne. He claimed we were all too tired to perform a proper Angola class so just let us play for half an hour, before giving us a talk. I understood nothing, and thought maybe Gabriel deserved another chance at teaching.

In the evening, Sena's group gave a show, which incorporated Makulele, and Puxada de Rede (Pulling of the net). This is where people dress up as sailors and act out the pulling of their fishing net whilst singing some sad songs about a lost colleague. Though this was the first time I had seen it, I was to become very familiar with this over the months.

A party at the farm followed the show, and Brie needed saving from both sets of Muzenza and Senzala guys, who were expressing some characteristic Brazilian, womanising charm. She even admitted it was starting to annoy her now.

Though I always enjoyed the weekend trips and Batizados, the next one wasn't scheduled for several weeks, so it was another chance to get into the routine of Rio training again. Unfortunately, this was interrupted with Mestres Ramos and Peixinho traveling, to New York and Europe respectively.

With the growth of Capoeira in both the US and Europe, this is now happening more and more, with Teachers who begin giving classes abroad keeping their contacts with their own Mestres, and group, and inviting them to events and to give classes. Gato himself was due to make one of his bi-annual trips to England in the next month.

Students of the Mestres therefore took classes. In Peixinho's case, this was usually Azeite, who would give a very similar lesson to that of his Mestre, in both style and content. Ramos' lessons were taken over by either Ana Sabia, one of his female professors, or a blue cord that simply became known as Brie's boyfriend, just because she liked him. Her flirting with him meant that his lessons became rather comedic, with a constant stream of "Isso, Formiguinha, Isso!" (That's it!) and then a nod when I got something correct. This certainly wasn't affecting my confidence though, as I thought I was playing as well as I had ever done, and finally reacting to my opponent's movements in the ways I had been taught. This confidence soon got me into trouble though. Gato had started to play me slightly harder as the weeks had gone on, and in his next lesson he didn't hold back.

First, I received a Martello in the arm, and then just seconds later, I was sitting on my backside after Gato had given me a bencão which knocked me three feet back, and about two feet high. As I looked down, it was like someone had tattooed a large foot onto my chest, and Gabriel soon laughed in my ear asking "why didn't you fall in negativa, stupid?"

If Gato's class hadn't given me enough bruising, Toni's class the next night certainly made sure I did. The class went well, with the usual good humour mixed in with the training. I partnered Samurai, as we did Quixada met with an entrance of Vigitiva. The roda then started, and several of Ramos' students had made the trip across Rio and added to the energy. Though I recognized Ana Sabia, I didn't recognize another purple cord that was playing a lot, and though he was quick, he lacked control in his kicks, and was continuously landing them off-balance. He soon bought my game however, and I was careful as he didn't slow his pace against me. His lack of subtlety allowed me to see many of his kicks, and I was trying to react in the ways Gato had taught me. As he did a Meu Lua de Compasso, I followed, but I didn't see his next kick as he landed a Pisao right on my chest, and I flew out the roda. The kick almost settled into the indent that Gato's had made the day before, though I think Gato had a size bigger foot. Fortunately, Gabriel wasn't there to ask me why I didn't fall the way I had been taught. Twice in two nights would have been too much, but I did feel some anger toward my opponent. I was wearing my yellow cord, and this, together with my basic game, should have been enough to tell him I was a mere beginner. There was certainly no need to go after me in this way, and I thought he had compromised his certain responsibility of being a Professor. However, I was glad it wasn't Meathead at the end of that leg!

Whilst training continued for Brie and I, Panda was still missing classes, and Gato was starting to lose patience. At his next lesson, Panda watched whilst complaining of more knee pains, but still managed to spend ten minutes kicking the kickbag at the end of the lesson. Gato, who always enjoyed a joke, then mimicked him limping from training, and threatened to change his name to Banana, because he appeared to bruise so easily, but this just dampened Panda's spirit further. He didn't even see the funny side of me groping Brie in class. We were training Banda da Costa, which involves felling a person by pushing their chest over a supporting leg, as I got frustrated with not pushing hard enough. The next time I mentally prepared not to 'wimp out', but as I pushed forward, I grabbed Brie's left breast, and then we just stood looking at each other before laughing. Gato said it was a different technique, but that maybe I should try it outside the roda.

Morning training was beginning to revolve more and more around Bimba's sequences. These eight, two person sequences were one of Bimba's greatest legacies of his teaching, and incorporated the basic movements of Capoeira Regional. Each morning we would finish our warm-up by performing all eight in a row, which I had now memorized since Lee and I had started doing this before. More movements Gato favoured, such as rasteira de chão inevitably followed these, and then some kicks on the pad. Though tiring, this 'blood and guts' training was really beginning to help my game, but Gato had recently criticized me for playing too far outside, and this was something I needed to work on. Capoeira is only a game when the players have to react to each other's movements, and by playing outside too often, i.e. far away from your opponent, your movements can become meaningless, as no reaction is necessary. However, I did take comfort from the fact that Gato based this criticism on a game I had played with one of Peixinho's blue cords, whose legs were so long, it was hard not to play outside.

With our next weekend trip about to come, more people were arriving from the UK. Ruchi was a doctor who trained with Pedro's group, along with Rob and the engaged couple, Sky and Conrad. Medusa, so called because of his dreadlocks, was also about to arrive, and I was pleased about this. Medusa was another student of my teacher, and had been on the trip to Amsterdam some months before. He was seen as the 'coolest' Capoeirista of our group. He had started training whilst living in Tokyo, and loved the acrobatic side of Capoeira. He also picked the movements up quickly, and moved well in the roda. With his dreadlocks, somersaults and baggy clothes, it was easy to see why the group saw him the way they did in England.

With the amount of students now in Rio, Gato decided to move morning training to the Academy in Leme, and Medusa immediately gave me some confidence by telling me how much my game had improved. I had to admit with the amount of work I had put in, if it hadn't improved at all I might have considered quitting. Though still with no rhythm, and definitely no Martello, I was certainly more balanced in my movements. I had also recently played the game of my short Capoeira life against Professor Ninho at a meeting in Barra da Tijuca, and felt good. I did seem to be developing some Eczema on my ankles however, and this was causing me great pain when people attempted a rasteira. A minor problem for now, but it was rather perplexing, as I had never had eczema before.

Chapter Six

Vamos Pedir o Axe
(Let's ask for the energy...Mestre Acordeon)

Brazil is famous for numerous things, the sun, the beaches, samba, carnival, the Amazon, the women, and many more. However, it also has one other quality that the whole world knows it for, and that is football. Through winning five world cups, the yellow shirts of the national football team have made the country infamous, but the style in which they have won these competitions have made the team loved. Brazil has always produced players of immense skill, and flamboyance, and I was eager to see more. After seeing a mere weekend player on the local pitches of Flamengo flick a ball over his, and his opponents head, with the style of Pele, I was desperate to see the professionals. The Carioca teams of Flamengo, Botafogo, Fluminense and Vasco da Gama gave me that chance each weekend, and I became a regular visitor to the Maracanã stadium.

Though the matches were full of fouls, and poor defending, the skill level was high, as was the entertainment provided by the crowd. Their banners and flags would literally cover hundreds of seats, and their chants would fill the massive stadium, even if their numbers didn't. If their team scored, they would often run down rows of seats in pure ecstasy, and I saw more than one seat be beaten in frustration when things weren't going so well. Classicos (derby matches) were always a special event, and seeing Vasco's star striker Romario score a hatrick against Flamengo in front of 75,000 spectators was special. I was particularly glad I hadn't sat with the Flamengo fans, who began rioting when Vasco's fourth goal was scored. Romario was only 5 feet 4, and in football, as in Capoeira, I always favoured the smaller players.

    With Gato's family supporting Botafogo, I had chosen them as my team, but actually watched more of Fluminense, who had the best season of all the Carioca teams, qualifying for the semi-finals of the Championship. I was more interested in watching specific players however. Each team seemed to include one, or maybe two, players who were the 'stars' of the team, and it was these that excited the crowd. Petkovic was Flamengo's Yugoslav star, Botafogo had Rodrigo in midfield, Roger caressed the ball beautifully for Fluminense and Vasco obviously had Romario. He was the biggest character in the entire league, and though a former World Footballer of the Year, was known for his wild ways, which were documented in the paper each day.

With the football and training taking up more of my time, it seemed that Panda was becoming concerned for me. As he took the new arrivals to a market and I went off to football, he found it necessary to give me some advice. "There's more to life than football and training Neil". "Really", I responded, "what's that then?" I managed to bite my tongue over him giving advice on how to live when all he had done since he arrived was moan and skip classes. Panda had proven himself to be overweight, lazy, and at times, not of sound mind. He was also prone to being highly disrespectful, and told us that he wanted to return to Brazil, but definitely didn't want to stay with Gato again, claiming that Teresopolis suited him far better. As Gato had taken him into his home, I found his attitude rather strange, to say the least.

However, this wasn't enough for Panda. Whilst we ate lunch with Medusa and Rob one afternoon, Panda claimed he had no reason to respect Mestre Peixinho. We were aghast as Panda returned to his now irritating story of how he had trained in Martial Arts for twenty years, and therefore he should be respected. We could do nothing but laugh, and the next day at breakfast, Gato was again stirring the mixture with images of Panda doing sit-ups at 6 years old. Panda took it badly and walked away moaning of Gato's attitude. Though we tried to keep the peace with Panda's attitude, it was becoming more and more difficult, and it was yet to come to a head. Medusa was later to find out what Panda was capable of.

With Panda's lack of humour, I was lucky to have Gabriel, who was very much the opposite, laid back, relaxed and always willing to share a joke. Having said this, there wasn't really much for Gabriel to be stressed about. His days consisted of school until midday, and then practicing his guitar in the afternoon by the swimming pool. This gave us plenty of time for Portuguese lessons, but this new attempt lasted as long as the first. The inevitable petty arguments meant I learnt little, and Gabriel was fired for the second, but not yet final, time. He did have something to teach me however, and when I came home from training one evening with a child's football game, his eyes lit up.

Fütebol de Botão (button football) is an incredibly simplistic game that is traditionally played by Brazil's children. A controlling button is used between the forefinger and thumb in order to push two teams of smaller buttons. These maneuver a small cubic ball around a pitch, to the general rules of football. Gabriel had played since his childhood, and we were soon having regular games, even having favoured 'players'. My star button, a small player of course, was painted in the colours of Fluminense, and scored the only goal in our opening match. The purchasing of a table and new goalposts gave Panda new concerns over my behaviour, and Medusa certainly didn't have the patience for the game, but Gabriel and I had found the perfect way to resolve our bickering.

Gabriel wasn't the only one to have played since his childhood however, and we were soon introduced to a new kind of 'Mestre'. Beatrice's father was now an aging man, but had played in goal for Botafogo in his youth, and grew quite excited as he saw button football turning into a regular Brazil versus England 'friendlies'. Gabriel and I were soon in awe though, as he pushed me aside and hit a blistering shot from the halfway line into the goal. Was there any side to football that Brazilians were bad at?

Though training was continuing as normal, my problem with 'eczema' was becoming worse, but was soon to be explained. Brie and I were due round at Gato's for morning training as normal at 7am, but we received a nasty shock as we awoke. I ran into Brie's room covered in small black insects, and it didn't take long to find plenty of them on her too. We had a flea problem, and the mixture of the filthy pool, and an even filthier Black, was the cause. For some reason the pests had taken a liking to my room over Brie's and my ankles and waist were covered in lumps. All the blankets in the house seemed to have been made into nice flea homes, and thus a major operation was needed.

Brie and I took some bandanas and placed them over our mouths as we covered the house in flea killer, and took all the blankets outside. Though enjoying the feeling of looking like assassins, we didn't step outside the front gate for fear of being seen as an opposing bandit. If we had trouble dealing with fleas, then I think Rio's gangland may have been a step too far for us.

After a couple of nights, it was obvious that our operation had failed, and we decided to speak to Peixinho. Though he found it immensely funny, he was generally sympathetic and said he would call in some pest control and clean the pool and dog. Brie and I were happy with this, until we found out that Mario was the pest controller, and as we went round to collect our things to move out for the night, there he was in his combat gear. Flip flops, jogging trousers, T-shirt and a backpack full of Puga (flea) killer. He looked like the bounty hunter from Star Wars, and I had visions of him flying over the house spraying his gun. We decided to leave him to it however, as we had another weekend Capoeira trip planned.

Though Rio is a beautiful city (its nickname is 'cidade maravilhosa'- the Marvelous City) surrounded by mountains and beaches, and overlooked by Jesus himself, it still has the problems of other cities. Traffic creates polluted air, and many areas are renowned for crime. Cariocas are fortunate, however, in that they only have to travel a short distance north, south or west before they are in another paradise.

Arraial do Cabo is a three hour drive from Rio de Janeiro and with so many gringos to take care of, Gato hired a minibus for the drive. The trip was to last for five days, and was to include seminars and classes with Mestres Gato, Touro, Paulinho Sabia, Toni and Elias. Gato had organized the trip in conjunction with the Capoeira Brasil group who were based in the small town, and it made a perfect location. The local residents were friendly, and the beaches spectacular.

Capoeira Brasil have a close relationship with Senzala. The three leading Masters of the group, Mestres Boneco, Paulinho Sabia and Paulao, all trained with Senzala in the past, and the friendships have remained strong. As with Cordao de Ouro, meetings are regularly shared and enjoyed together, as was the case in Arrail.

Our hotel was located directly in front of the main beach, and I was to share a room with Medusa, Rob and Panda. With the arrival of Michelle, a New Zealander who also trained with Pedro in Edinburgh, there were now two distinct groups, the girls and the guys. As well as I was getting on with Brie, I was glad to stay with the guys, and I think Brie appreciated her new female company.

After settling in, the afternoon was to be spent on a boat trip round the expensive residences that surround Cabo Frio, which gave Pedro the perfect chance to embarrass me. Pedro's sense of humour naturally honed in onto people's misfortunes and so it was that I was given my nickname. Just two weeks before I had spent a day on Beatrice's brother's boat, sailing round Sugar Loaf Mountain, before heading for

Copocabana and Ipanema beaches. By the time we reached the second beach however, my stomach was trying to remember better times, and the inevitable happened. As Pedro told the story to the whole group he started calling me Raul (pronounced How-all), which corresponds to the noise people make when they vomit. Capoeiristas down the years had been nicknamed with reference to their style of play, or maybe a mannerism they had, or the way they looked, but there it was, for the rest of my Capoeira life I was to be known as someone who threw up off the side of a boat.

The name stuck and gave numerous chances for jokes as the week progressed, especially as the boat trip was followed by another just two days later. Fortunately, the stomach behaved on both occasions. Medusa even suggested I try and create a new cartwheel, as the Portuguese for cartwheel is Aû, therefore the Raul Au was awaiting creation (and still is I might add).

The day ended in the usual fashion, as we all took part in classes taught by Mestres Touro and Gato. Though I had seen his group at his batizado, I had never seen Touro teach, and his style was certainly different from what I was used to. He concentrated his lesson on two things. Firstly, Aûs that ended crashing on top of your opponent, and secondly, moving to the floor and always coming up with a kick, usually the pushing kick of Chapa. In the evening roda, Touro showed his playing style, along with his eccentricity, as he tied his T-shirt round his head and crashed his Aûs with a large roar. Whether you appreciated his style or not, it was certainly entertaining to watch, as even Pedro was struggling to avoid the unusual attacks.

The daytimes were largely spent on the beach, and here Medusa found his home. A Brazilian was always at hand to show him a new flip, and Medusa was thirsty for the knowledge. With his dreadlocks flying, and the backdrop of white sand, it certainly made a good picture and Beatrice clicked away all week.

The arrival of the weekend saw the arrival of the remaining Mestres, and I was eagerly awaiting the lesson of Paulinho Sabia. He seemed to move round the roda like he was walking on a thin layer of ice, and this, matched with his relaxed, but at times very quick, movements made him a joy to watch. His lesson involved practicing Aû, whilst controlling the descent to the floor, and ending in negativa. This requires strength, and great control of the body, and though I had worked plenty on the first of these, the second would take more time to come. The roda was the best yet as the newly arrived Mestres, and their students, added greatly to the energy, and though Beatrice complemented me on my games, I was unhappy with the way I played.

I often found myself still playing as quickly as possible, and my still stiff ginga was making it difficult for me to fake any movement to my opponent. It was often disheartening after playing badly in a roda, and it sometimes led you to doubt whether your game was improving at all, even with all the training. I often found this was tiredness, or a case of trying too hard, and then tensing up in the roda.

Though I always enjoyed playing in the rodas, the way I played would always affect my mood after, and usually far too much. Capoeira is there to be enjoyed, and sometimes with this over-analysis of my games, I lost this point. However, in my defense, I was training highly intensively, and thus it was highly natural to think about my game, and its development, in detail. Even when I did play badly, if the energy of a roda was good, then this could change anyone's mood. The atmosphere after a good roda can often resemble that of the end of a good party, with everyone shaking hands and hugging like long lost friends. The adrenaline provided by the music and games can be hugely unifying, as if everyone involved knows something the outside world doesn't, and is much better off for it.

Medusa also tended to analyse his own games, and I lost count of the amount of times he told me how badly he had played, even when I thought he hadn't at all. Though he was good at giving others confidence, he often lacked it in himself, but this made a pleasant change from the many egotistical Capoeiristas I met, and the numerous people who thought they knew much more than they really did. I always appreciated Medusa's humbleness.

The trip continued with more banter within the group, and some integration with the local Capoeira group. They invited us to a party, where a rather drunken roda was formed, followed by a Samba de roda. A samba de roda is simply a circle of people, and like a roda of capoeira, two people enter and dance samba, until someone buys the dance. Mestre Elias, whose enormous smile provided an even greater feel-good atmosphere, led this one. As is common in these rodas, many of the songs were created on the spot, and would refer to the people involved, though usually to the women. Three great Brazilian loves mixed: music, samba and women.

The final day of the trip was the hottest so far, and thus a trip to the beach was in order. As Toni's students played samba, and Doboru showed me that it wasn't just Brazilian males who could play football, the holiday atmosphere was completed with beer and fresh fish being passed around. Soon another roda was made, and the sound of berimbaus complimented with those of the waves. Playing Capoeira on the beach is always difficult, as sand flies in the eyes, and balance becomes more difficult. However, the roda had a party feel to it, and the energy kept it going for two solid hours, before the final group photos were taken and the minibus beckoned.

Chapter Seven

Ie viva meu Mestre
(Ie long live my Master...Popular)

With the Favella relatively free of fighting, and after Mario's 'expert' de-fleaing, Peixinho's house was feeling the most homely it had since Brie and I had moved in. Our landlord had started to spend more time at the house, as the rise in gringos had also meant a large rise in business for Peixinho's berimbaus, and he housed his workshop in our basement. Brie and I felt honoured to be able to watch such a Mestre at work as we made our dinner of an evening. Peixinho would often work till late at night, and was known for his perfectionist ways. I would often hear him testing his berimbaus for sound, before working on them more and then testing them again.

There is a lot of work in making a berimbau. It is composed of the beriba (a stick of wood about 5 feet in length), the kebasa (a hollowed gourd from a tree), the wire, a caxixi (a shaker), a pacqueta (a stick used to hit the wire) and a stone or a coin, which is pushed against the wire to make the desired sound. The size of the Kebasa decides whether the berimbau becomes a gunga (with a loud deep sound), a viola (a small kebasa which carries a higher pitched sound) or a media (in between the two). Peixinho wasn't happy until each part of the berimbau was just the way he wanted it, and the ones he used for his rodas had a great sound to them. I was always especially intrigued by his main berimbau, which was white in colour, but looked very old. Brie and I imagined what rodas it had seen down the years.

Despite the dangers that surrounded living in a Favella, the local residents were always friendly with us, and with this in mind, Michelle and Ruchi decided it was safe enough to join Brie and myself. Their cooking skills were certainly superior to Brie's and mine, and their easygoing ways suited me. However, Black didn't appreciate their ways, and shortly after he scared the new arrivals one too many times, he was moved downstairs to the basement on a permanent basis. Though I had to feel some sympathy for him, he scared me too whenever I arrived at the house. It also meant I didn't have to calm him down each time I entered the house, so I was by no means devastated

With Peixinho's house now having three girls, soon to be nicknamed the Raulinhas, and me, Gato's house was the opposite, housing Medusa, Panda, Rob and obviously Gabriel. Pedro had now returned to face the coldness of Scotland once again. Tensions were rising in each, but for different reasons.

Though individually I got on with all the girls, they were becoming inseparable, and their conversation often ranged from pregnancy to Peixinho's tight backside. Surprisingly I had little to say on these subjects, and thus I became increasingly quiet at mealtimes. They knew this, and even tried to organize nights out where there was something for all, as I didn't share their love of trance music. However, despite their efforts, it was always a case of being three girls, and one guy, and I never could find Peixinho's rear sexy.

Medusa was also having problems, namely with Panda's temperament, and found it hard to bite his tongue when Panda exaggerated, or started preaching. Things came to a head after Rob had left to return to Scotland. He had been the peacemaker of the group, and with him gone, Medusa had to spend more time alone with Panda, whose claims were becoming more and more farcical. One afternoon he claimed to speak eight languages, which Medusa responded with a blunt "I'm sorry but stop lying, I don't believe you". However, just two days later Panda's behaviour went too far and when Medusa refused to stop channel flicking, Panda jumped on top of him, grabbing the television controller. Gabriel sat in disbelief, as Medusa told Panda what a child he was and how glad he was that he was leaving soon.

I was to witness Panda's growing strangeness just a few nights later, as well as the worst Favella violence I had heard. I was spending more and more time with Gabriel and

Medusa, and one evening we had decided to watch a film. As we sat in Gato's lounge, suddenly we heard shots ring out from the street outside. They were extremely loud, and following Gabriel's advice, Medusa and I were soon underneath the table. The Favella opposite was firing directly at the rival bandits who had ventured out of their homes and onto Gato's street. We could hear shouting in front of the house and when a grenade exploded, we knew this was very serious, and soon enough, the sounds of the Police guns could be heard. For fifteen minutes the three of us lay on the floor as shot followed shot. However, it was soon interrupted as a drum in the house soon started to sound. It had to be Panda, and where was he playing, but right by the window in front of the shots.

"Wow, did you see that?" he asked rather matter-of-factly. Gabriel couldn't believe Panda had been so stupid and responded immediately, "Are you stupid or something, man? Standing next to a window with all that shooting". "Ah they weren't gonna hit me" responded Panda in a thicker than normal Scottish accent, "and anyhow, I could dodge a bullet anyway". This was the last straw for Medusa, who simply laughed as Panda told us about being shot at in Dundee on a regular basis, and then boring us with what guns he thought they were using outside. What made Panda believe anyone would believe his childish claims I'm not entirely sure, but risking his life in such a stupid way was stubbornness taken too far. He had lost any respect he had left from any of us, and, sadly, we were now looking forward to his imminent return to Scotland.

With the good atmosphere of the group, as well as the numbers, receding after the trip to Arraial de Cabo, training was fast becoming our sole unifying activity. I still regularly partnered Brie, in the morning and evenings, and our desire to train was as strong as ever. Medusa, though often lazy about going to class, worked hard when he got there, and I enjoyed working with him and his good technique. Panda had stopped even coming to many classes claiming he needed a holiday. Michelle and Ruchi were newer to Capoeira, and didn't appreciate Peixinho's rodas, which were still as intimidating as ever. Medusa also felt uncomfortable here, after receiving a fast Martello to his eye from Cutia in his first lesson. Though Peixinho had warned Cutia, Medusa was never to feel relaxed in these rodas, but it wasn't to be the last hard Martello he was to take.

Ramos continued to give good lessons, and with Gato teaching in England for a month, killer Tuesdays and Thursdays were no longer, and we certainly had more energy for his classes. This was just as well, as in his next class I was to partner the Purple cord who had kicked me at Toni's class weeks earlier. Ramos enjoyed using techniques that ended in entering onto your opponent and giving a cabeçada (a head butt) or a throw. This particular lesson, he showed us a sequence that included the throw Vigitiva, and my partner was surprisingly helpful to me, before throwing me five feet across the room. I simply laughed and tried to take his advice as I put as much power into my technique as possible.

It was Toni's classes that were giving us the most enjoyment now, however. The girls loved Toni's openhearted way, and after the trip to Arraial, I found his students as friendly as ever. However, one class did split our group once again. Toni was giving a course in Minais Gerais, so his student, Professor Lobo, was to give the class. Medusa and I exchanged looks as he handed out a candle to everyone. The idea of moving round the candle certainly raised a smile on my face, but when we started to do this to Harry Krishna music, I avoided Medusa's face like the plague deliberately for fear of showing a lack of respect and laughing. I appreciated the creativeness of Lobo, but after an hour, I had lost interest in the training, and was beginning to question the point. I began to think that the end of class chat would prove interesting.

It certainly did, and it went as I expected. The girls found the class "amazing", and enjoyed every minute. They guessed my reaction, and when I questioned the point of the class, it raised a smile. Fortunately, the girls and I agreed to disagree on many things, and the most heated any argument ever got with any of them was with Brie, and whether Alanis Morrisette's song really is ironic (it clearly isn't!). Fortunately I had Medusa who shared my opinion, and we laughed with the returning Gato, the next day.

With training taking up my evenings, and most mornings, the rest of the day was spent relaxing, and much of the time with Gabriel and our button football table. Our matches were quickly, and sadly thought the others, becoming of a high standard, and the ball was being moved round the pitch with a fair amount of skill. Our shooting had also improved, and the top corner was often found with blistering pace. Much to Gabriel's annoyance, I had made good progress in our early games, and my star Fluminense striker was top scorer as I went on a three game winning streak.

A 5-0 defeat sent Gabriel into near depression however, and the loss to a mere 'gringo' was an obvious insult to him. I suspected he had been practicing with his school friends when he came back in the following games, winning two of the next three, or maybe even taking lessons from his Grandfather. The pettiness even went as far as Gabriel claiming I had stolen his favourite striker, when really he had been my player all along. I did manage to steal his Romario button though, who became a steadying influence on my midfield.

These games had to come to an end however, as all the gringos were planning to travel. After I had spent four months training in Rio, with the exception of the weekend events, I felt it was time to spend some time seeing Capoeira elsewhere, and also felt the group needed some time apart. It was therefore decided that Medusa and I were to travel to São Paulo and spend time at the legendary Mestre Suassuna academy during his batizado week, before flying to Fortaleza to experience some of the beaches of the North East. The girls had decided to travel to the City of Recife, also in the North East, and meet up with Brie's Mestre, who was traveling with her group from Canada.

Chapter Eight

Quem vem la, Sou eu, Berimbau bateu, Capoeira Sou eu
(Who goes there, It's me, the berimbau called, Capoeira it's me)

Coaches in Brazil are big business, and with so many people using them to travel from one city to another, comfort is taken to an infinitely higher level than in England. Medusa and I decided to travel to São Paulo by Leito, the most luxurious coach available, and we settled into our armchair-like seats and stole some sleep on the five hour ride. The disadvantage of us traveling this way was that we arrived at the unsociable hour of 5am, and the rumours of São Paulo being far more dangerous than Rio (many Paulistas we met said the opposite), meant that carrying our bags around looking for a hotel was a nerve-racking experience. We soon found one however, and set up shop in a central part of São Paulo.

How central is hard to say, as the city is a sprawling metropolis. Our early impressions weren't good, and as the first page of our guidebook recommended not coming in the first place, our expectations were low. As we ventured out on a Sunday morning, we saw why. São Paulo is Brazil's industrial heartland, and is very different from Rio. Where Rio has beaches and mountains, São Paulo is a concrete mesh of dirty, old decaying buildings and its Favellas stretch out for many miles. The density of traffic, and the problems with trying to house over twenty million people, makes for polluted air mixed with the already humid climate. During the day the streets become a mass market, with music sellers competing for custom with their sound systems, and clothes sellers vying for a sale.

Medusa and I started to speak to some locals, and we found out that São Paulo is actually loved by many of its residents, and has many fine parks, restaurants and nightclubs. However, to reach them you need a car, and so we laid back and watched cheap Brazilian TV, in what was to feel like our prison of a room, as the rain poured down outside.

Even with our low expectations of São Paulo, Medusa and I had agreed to stay for nine days, and there was one reason for this, Mestre Suassuna. Suassuna had meant to teach at both the Liga Mundo de Capoeira and Minais Gerais meetings I had attended, but had pulled out through illness on both occasions. If he wasn't going to come to me, then I obviously had to go to him.

Though from the state of Bahia, Suassuna had moved south in the 1960s, and as Group Senzala grew in Rio, his group, Cordao de Ouro (Golden Cord), grew likewise in São

Paulo. Under his direction, his group grew in reputation and size, and it was now one of the biggest, and most respected, with schools all around the world. The group concentrated on a more regional style, but Medusa was excited at the prospect of finding some more acrobatic players than in Senzala.

The main academy was based in the Santa Cecilia district, and I was particularly excited when I saw that most days saw six lessons take place. Our first was Monday afternoon, and as Suassuna narrowed his eyes at Medusa and myself as we walked up the stairs, I spoke my best and politest Portuguese to tell him who we were. He was clearly not the athlete he once was with a burgeoning stomach. However, I had seen enough older Mestres to know that they never lose their aura, and the same was true once more. Also, Suassuna was a small man and as always, this gave me more interest in his Capoeira and how he may have used this to his advantage.

Gato was a close friend of his and had already warned him of our arrival. We stepped into the academy and watched two players practicing the game of Miudinho. Medusa's eyes lit up as he whispered, "fuck, we've been here two minutes and we're seeing the best Capoeira we've ever seen". Miudinho is a game that Suassuna's students spend much time on, and is similar to Jogo de Dentro, with the berimbau toque being alike. There are sets of sequences that Suassuna created which are performed, and it was one of these that the players were practicing when Medusa and I arrived. The two students, who we later found out to be Kibe and Dennis, jumped over each other and caught their bodies with their hands, showing immense control, whilst combining their Meu Lua de Compassos expertly. It was the sheer flow that caused Medusa to make his remark.

The lessons themselves were no longer taken by Suassuna, who is in such demand he spends much of his time traveling whilst organising the academy, but by Professor Tourinho. He had injured his foot and thus had to hobble to the front of the class to give the warm-up, and then bark out his orders for the lesson. The first lesson was to set the format for the week. The first thirty minutes were everything, and everyone would ginga, jump, ginga and jump again until sweat was dripping all over the floor. This was then followed with kick after kick, until everyone breathed a sigh of relief as we did movements going down the academy. This meant that only so many people could practice at once, and thus most people were able to catch their breath and grab a much needed drink.

The class's blue cords led the lines. The Cordao de Ouro cording system is different to Senzalas, and Medusa and I were never to fully comprehend it. Our best guess was that green was beginner, yellow was someone not to mess with, and blue meant the person could be anywhere between brilliant, and very ordinary. The higher students seemed to have cords with a mixture of colours. Several students struck us immediately however. Boca Rica (rich mouth) and Dennis were blue cords, and played well, but Kibe seemed the most talented. Though he also had a blue cord, he led most movements in the lessons and would spend literally his whole day there. His mixture of balance, pace, control and strength gave him a game that was already good, but had the obvious potential to be quite brilliant.

The slightly short lessons would always end with a particularly long roda, and we were told that this was because of the preparations for the upcoming batizado, which would take place at the end of the week. We were to witness many of these, as the group practiced their African dancing and Makulele (which was already excellent under Suassuna's tuition), whilst the unlucky ones made cord after cord.

Though the lessons were short, they were exhausting and Medusa and I were certainly feeling the strain after a few days. However, the long rodas, and often few people, meant we were playing game after game, and learning each time. It was exactly what we needed to put into practice the training we had been doing. However, all these games also had their downside. Suassuna's students seemed intent on taking their opponent down with either a rasteira or a throw, and this was leading to some messy games, and highly bruised ankles. Medusa and I were comparing our shins after each roda to see who had been hacked most, and there seemed to be one main culprit. Though we never found out her name, one particular girl was obsessed with giving rasteira, and mostly very badly.

Her foot was often imprinted on Medusa's shin, or mine and we would smile at each other when one of us stepped up to play her.

This slightly aggressive play came to a head in one of Medusa's games. He was playing an experienced player, who was again trying to throw him at any opportunity. Medusa decided to hit back and protect himself, and gave a bencão, pushing his opponent off his feet and out of the roda. The game continued, but only briefly, as Dennis soon bought the game. Three fast Martellos to Medusa's head were his 'punishment', for daring to kick a Brazilian. Medusa was fuming, as it seemed they could pick on us, but never the other way round, and it turned out that his initial opponent was actually a more experienced player than him. Having seen it, I had to agree, and thought Dennis' treatment was far too severe. Medusa's headache lasted two days.

Outside of training, São Paulo was living up to the nightmare we had thought possible. Medusa would often make himself miserable by talking of his girlfriend he had left at home. The lack of access to entertainment meant more watching of cheap Brazilian television. Only the constant re-iteration of Monty Python jokes kept our moods up, as well as the talk of out next destination, the relaxing North East. We both agreed an afternoon from training was needed and had been saving something just for this occasion.

No matter how many times Medusa had read the guide book, the lack of things to do never sounded any better, and we had spent some afternoons in the local cinemas, which, like many buildings, hadn't changed since the 1950s. However, we had soon watched every film available to us, and so it was that we ended up at São Paulo's top tourist attraction, a snake farm. After the hour-long bus journey there, half an hour looking at different snakes in glass cages, and then twenty minutes searching for the ones hiding underneath rocks, we were ready for the hour journey home on an air free bus, which spent most of its time in traffic. Many people at the academy had told us we were wrong about the City, and it was actually filled with delights. After this fiasco though, we just refused to believe it, and we had reached a new low point outside the academy for the week. However, we still had the Batizado to look forward to, and just two days before we were given a taster.

We had spent our fifth day much like the previous ones, in the academy ginga-ing, jumping, kicking, sweating and playing. Only this day we had also done many movements involving Ponte (bridge). These movements are used a lot in Miudinho, and thus the academy would train them over and over, and far more than Senzala. I struggled, as Tourinho attempted to push my body into positions it never thought possible, never mind comfortable. Medusa was more than happy, and his more 'natural' Capoeira ways shone through.

The evening was to be spent at a street roda, which promised to be slightly special with the arrival of many Mestres and teachers from all over Brazil. The Academies blue cords showed off many of their acrobatics movements, and the games were fast, and of a high standard. However, they were soon given a lesson of their own as Professor Esquilo (squirrel) entered the roda. Medusa and I had never seen anything like it, as he kicked and flipped his tiny frame as if on fast forward and all right next to his opponent. Medusa had heard about him before, and even after watching just one game, whispered in my ear again, "That was worth all the hassles of São Paulo". I had to agree, and Esquilo's technique made me think back to Tourneiro, but I didn't want to compare them, just remember them, and their sheer talent.

As the roda continued, and Medusa and I prayed for Esquilo to buy another game, some games were becoming aggressive. One player in particular wasn't holding back with his kicks, but when the girl who had been kicking Medusa's ankles and mine all week, finally did a good rasteira, he seemed to lose all control. Medusa and I believed in the darkness her opponent thought she was a man, and he struck out with his fists, and punched her right in the face, before someone pushed him away. As he left the roda however, the girl came back and kicked him in the leg, before running away in a fit of tears.

Medusa had found out the hard way not to touch someone with many friends in the roda (unfortunately he only had me, and I wasn't going after anyone who kicked him!), and so it was here too. Each time the player came back to play in the roda, a whole line of people queued up to teach him a lesson, and it didn't take long before he was rising to the bait. Two more hard games later, his fists were flying again, this time at Boca Rica, and Suassuna banished him from the roda.

With it being arranged by Suassuna and his group, the batizado was, perhaps unsurprisingly, the most organized I went to in Brazil. Everything took place on a stage in a large theatre that was packed with parents and students alike. The African fire dance was highly impressive, and the Makulele ended with two students crashing swords to create flashes in the darkness. Suassuna then staged a berimbau play-off with two of his students. As the two competed, playing complicated toques, Suassuna then entered and began playing behind his back and then with the berimbau upside down. With his small frame, cheeky smile and wobbling belly Suassuna was the natural 'joker in the pack', and played his part superbly well, leaving to a thunderous applause. It was almost too enjoyable though, and as expected, the slightly drawn out Puxada de rede was started, with groans from Medusa and myself.

The roda was then started, and despite some of the lead singers not fully recognizing the fact they were holding microphones and therefore didn't need to shout to be heard, it had good energy. We watched as many of the people we had been training with received their new cords, and played against a mixture of Mestres and teachers. Much to our disappointment, Esquilo played just twice. I did get speaking to a visiting student however, and he happened to be from Fortaleza, our next stop. He told us that he trained with the best Capoeirista he knew, Mestre Espirro Mirim, also from Cordão de Ouro. I recognized the name as being one of many that Gato had given me before we left, and made a note to look him up.

The end of the batizado signaled the nearness of the end of our time in São Paulo. After sitting through another rainy day in our room, the city had one final trick up its sleeve for us. As we turned up at the airport, desperate for some clean air and a beach, we realized we were exactly twenty-four hours late for our flight. The extra charge wasn't nearly as painful as the realization that we had spent a whole extra day in what Medusa termed as "hell on earth". Despite the fantastic Capoeira, I couldn't disagree.

Fortaleza is the capital of the Brazilian state of Ceará, and lies a three hour flight north of São Paulo. With Brazilian's industrial capital being famous for its size, smog, multicultural population and, well, its industry, Fortaleza and its surrounding area is famous for its beaches, idyllic towns, undeveloped villages and the music of Forro. Medusa actually thought that São Paulo's claustrophobic atmosphere was sending him mentally insane, and when he failed to laugh at another Monty Python reference ("Are you the Popular Peoples Front of Judea?"), I realized that he needed the change of scenery as much as I did.

I soon realized, however, that we had very different agendas planned. Whereas my rather obsessive way, made me want to find Mestre Espirro Mirim as soon as possible, Medusa was keen to skip off to a small town with a beach and relax. We decided to discuss our differing opinions over a night out, and here we were quickly introduced to the women of the North East. Though our dislike of Forro music discouraged us to visit the main nightclubs, we found plenty of bars in the Iraçema area. Drink followed drink, as Medusa and I found ourselves relaxing to our newfound laid-back city. We had met a Canadian girl, Chantal, in our hotel and she had joined us, and was soon remarking how she had never seen two men get so much attention. She was right. We sat at a table in the middle of the bar, and literally every girl's head in the bar was facing us. It was almost unnerving, and I felt like a mixture of alien and celebrity, as my blond hair and blue eyes, together with Medusa's light eyes and red dreadlocks, contrasted so deeply with everyone around us. As Chantal went to the toilet, Medusa read my mind, "We're coming back here without her tomorrow, right?"

Chantal had managed to persuade me that a trip to the small town of Jericoacoara was a good idea, and thus Medusa was happy. We agreed to just a few days there before returning to see Mestre Espirro. We were to leave in two days, which left us a further night in Fortaleza, and Medusa and I knew exactly what we were going to do with it.

Chantal had decided to have an early night, as we went for a delicious meal in a nearby restaurant. The nightlife of Iraçema has conglomerated in one small area, and it was just a short walk from the restaurants to the bars and clubs. We tried a couple of bars, but with our journey the next day in mind, we tried to limit what we were drinking. Brazil's national drink is Caipirinha, which consists of cachaça (Brazilian rum) mixed with ice, lime and sugar. Perhaps unsurprisingly, they are generally made strong, and just two or three can start to make a night quite forgettable. I always preferred them made with vodka, but this night we decided to stick to beer, which is always served ice cold.

The night seemed far busier than the previous one, and most of the bars were close to full by midnight. We decided to return to the bar we had sat in the previous night, and this too was busier than the night before. Once again it felt as if someone had given us Tom Cruise masks, as every female head in the bar turned toward us. A Danish friend in Rio had told me the best way to practice speaking Portuguese he knew was chatting up women. It sounded a reasonable excuse, if one was needed, to me and we were soon 'practicing our Portuguese' with some local girls over some drinks. However, after an hour I realised Medusa had gone. Knowing he was determined to stay loyal to his girlfriend, I knew he would still be in the bar, and though it was still crowded, it didn't take long to find him. He was doing what he later called his Ricky Martin impression, which meant he danced in an extremely cheesy manner whilst being surrounded by women. I gave it my best attempt, but I think Medusa may have been practicing his impression in a mirror before, as he seemed a natural.

The girls were showing us how to 'shake the ass' properly though. With the prominence of Samba in Brazil, girls seem to learn from an early age how to dance so provocatively, but so well. We were given a good lesson, but after some time, and becoming suspicious of some of their motives, we needed to leave the increasingly attaching girls behind, and call it a night. I had heard too many stories from tourists who had been drugged and robbed to be totally naïve and thus Medusa and I were careful. However, we promised each other never to forget the night when we felt a small amount of celebrity fame.

The bus journey to Jericoacoara (or Jeri as it is popularly known) takes seven hours, but is then supplemented by a forty-minute truck ride over the sand dunes that surround it. The town consisted of two roads (it has grown to almost four since), made of sand, with a large beach at the end, a few guest houses, a couple of bars and a small club used for Forro. Medusa had found his paradise, and when we went to the beach the next day, I thought I had too. It seemed that every child in the town played Capoeira, and at sunset each night, a roda would take place on the beach, bringing together all the Capoeiristas in the town.

Our days soon became a routine of having breakfast, wandering down to the beach, and training Capoeira in between drinking juices. Medusa was finding the local children experts on flipping around, and then finally got me spinning on my hand. We would then take part in the evening roda, which became quite dangerous after about twenty minutes as the sun was gradually swallowed by the sea, and it became near impossible to see the kicks coming your way. One of the better players used to wear dark brown trousers, which, allied with his dark skin, made him lethal once the sun had disappeared. I always thought he played more in the second half of the roda to make the most of his advantage, but this may have been paranoia on my behalf.

We soon made friends with the local Capoeira teacher, Wesley, and he was highly excited at having two gringos to teach, as well as being a hugely down to earth character. He concentrated much of his training on balance, and showed us his methods of improving this. He stood on one leg, holding his other in different position, and all without moving a muscle. It almost reminded me of ballet dancing, but the exercises obviously worked, as his ginga was always in perfect balance, and I never saw him lose control of his body once, whether upside down, or upright. Medusa was like a sponge when we trained with Wesley, and loved the new acrobatic sequences we were learning, as well as the lying under palm trees we did afterwards, which he seemed such a natural at.

The town was surrounded by sand dunes, and the locals loved to drive round them in their beach buggies. Though they all seemed to continuously play Dire Straits for a reason that we never discovered, we decided to hire one, and our driver gave us the thrills of a roller coaster as we drove down near vertical drops. I was more impressed with the way he actually knew where he was going. The horizon looked the same whichever way we looked, and as we drove over more dunes, they seemed to mould into one enormous desert.

The dunes did provide one other method of early evening entertainment however, and this centered around the particularly large pile of sand on the edge of the beach. The children would drag their sandboards to the top of the dune before zig-zagging their way down to the bottom. Though Medusa's first attempt saw him travel about two metres, he soon improved and after an hour was sliding down like the rest of them. Each time he arrived at the top more exhausted than the last as he climbed the steep hill, and he needed to be pulled up the final few yards more than once.

He was soon interrupted however, as everyone turned round to face a particularly strong looking character. He belonged on the front of a surfing magazine, with his tanned six-pack, and fair ponytail, and is how I imagined Peixinho (also a keen surfer) to look in his younger days. He had been stretching on his own for some time now, but the locals obviously knew him, and made way for his run up. He ran quickly the twenty metres to the edge of the dune before leaping off and somersaulting through the air, and back flipping down the sand. It was mighty impressive, and he was clearly a talented individual.

The excitement grew twenty minutes later when he pulled his sandboard from his bag. He began stretching again, and then waxed his board ferociously. Medusa and I sat back to watch the forthcoming entertainment as he approached the dune's edge once again. However, we weren't expecting comedy as halfway down he fell onto his backside, almost as fast as us, as we couldn't contain our chuckles.

The town would end the day by dancing Forro. I was told many times of how this dance actually originated from US soldiers after the Second World War organising dance evenings 'For all', with the music being supplied by an accordion and drum. With the Brazilian's pronunciation, this became Forro and a new dance and music tradition was begun. The music now usually consisted of a guitar, accordion, drum and tambourine, and allowed people to dance close, whilst spinning their partner around. This style is traditional to the North east, and thus the music could be heard everywhere, but after an hour or two, it would irritate us, and thus we began to claim some early nights in Jeri.

As Medusa and I agreed to ignore our plan of just staying a couple of days (I was somewhat dubious as to whether Medusa had any intention of keeping to it from the start), we decided to move into a new guest house. We couldn't resist the small chalets that resided on the quieter of the two roads. The chalets were spacious and clean, and the largest, but laziest dog I had ever met guarded the complex. If he made the fifty yard journey from the entrance to the chalets in an afternoon, it was a surprise, but he was never short for company, as people loved to lie and relax in the hammocks that surrounded the complex.

Our claiming of early nights was interrupted one night however, when we returned to the chalet from the club one night to a vicious and unexpected attack. It seemed that literally hundreds of flying ants had been breeding in a wall, and now they had burrowed their way through, covering the chalet and its contents. I was taken back to the mosquito war I had waged with Lee, and I took a flip-flop to the bathroom as Medusa searched for their base. He quickly found the hole and covered it with insect killer before sticking some tissue over it with toothpaste. I had no idea where the idea of toothpaste came from, but Medusa was convinced this would stop them burrowing through once again.

I had to admit I was slightly concerned over the amount of pleasure Medusa was taking in his work, but couldn't deny his effectiveness, as he joined me with a flip-flop. Anyone outside must have been extremely confused as to what was going on, as slap followed slap. They were on the floor, the beds, our bags, the mirrors, shelves, cupboards, and just about anything else they could land on. Some of the more clever ones decided to move to the ceiling, and we could do nothing about these, but others weren't so lucky. Half an hour of slapping later and we gave the room the all clear, before going to bed under the mosquito nets provided.

The next morning Medusa re-applied his toothpaste covering as the largest of the ants was once again burrowing through his wall. Our night's war games had covered the floor with dead bodies, and it felt strange to sweep up so many insects. I had never seen so many and couldn't help wondering how many more were waiting behind the wall of Colgate. I also couldn't help thinking of what an expert in pest killing I was becoming. If other Capoeiristas feared me like the mosquitoes and ants of Brazil were beginning to, I would have been a happy man.

After ten days based in the smallest of towns, it was time for Medusa and I to return to the City. He had a flight to Rio to catch and I had to keep my promise to see Mestre

Espirro Mirim, whose reputation had grown in my mind after speaking to the group in Jeri. Unfortunately, some milk, which was feeling the effects of the increasing heat, cost Medusa another night of Ricky Martin impersonations in Fortaleza, but he made his flight and I lost another partner for the time being.

Walking around Fortaleza, one can't help but feel a slight disappointment with it. It has long beaches, but these are mostly dirty and polluted, and it is currently building new apartments blocks and hotels, but with very limited style. The holidaying Paulistas and Southern Europeans that visit have provided the funds for this, and one can't help but feel an opportunity being slightly wasted. However, I now faced one of my biggest challenges since I had arrived in Brazil. I proposed resisting the city's stunning surrounding areas, and staying to train for the week.

I quickly managed to find Mestre Espirro's training times after talking with a student who happened to be wearing his T-shirt. This wasn't to be the first time I used this technique, and I looked forward to meeting the man himself. Though I had now heard so much about him, I had never seen Espirro before and had no idea what to expect, so when someone pointed me towards a tiny character that looked like he had escaped from the computer room, I was somewhat surprised. Though he was sitting, he seemed smaller than myself, and didn't have the muscles I was expecting. He also had a hint of a side parting, and though I had learned never to judge a book by its cover, I couldn't help wondering if I was really talking to the right person.

I explained to the friendly Mestre who I was, but was still wondering if this really could be "the best Cordao de Ouro Capoeirista" as I had been told. Capoeiristas come in all shapes and sizes, and people's styles are often reflected in this. I had seen players with legs that appeared longer than my entire body, and though I could learn things from watching them, I always preferred to watch smaller players, who couldn't rely on their reach to catch people. Instead they would have to develop the speed and agility to enter close to an opponent.

Espirro sat surrounded by his students. We were then sent to pick up some pads, and we were soon combining our kicks on them. I was to partner two students, and soon enough we were chatting about England and the Capoeira there. The North East obviously received many less foreign travelers than Rio, and I always found the locals to be friendly and inquisitive, as well as an excellent tool with which to practice my Portuguese.

After an hour, most of the class was sitting listening to Espirro, as I carried on training. One student sensed my disappointment and told me the next night was a better organised class, and not to miss it. He then practiced the most perfect handspin I had ever seen, before leaving to speak to his Mestre again.

Fortunately, this one student happened to be right and the next class was classic Cordao de Ouro training. Espirro exhausted us for half an hour with just movements in our ginga, and a smile came upon my face as we dodged imaginary kicks, and jumped around to a Mestre Toni CD. We then found a partner and dodged each other's Quixadas as quickly as possible, before forming the roda. Espirro took up a berimbau and created the energy by jumping around as he sung, and the games began. Gato had told me before that the style of Capoeira in Fortaleza was different to Rio, with more acrobatics and jumps, and now I saw it. There seemed to be less fight than in Rio, and the players' movements were nothing short of beautiful, as they span on their hands before entering with a fast kick. It was mesmerising to watch the perfect combinations the students were performing, and I compared it to watching twenty Esquilo wannabes. I played a few games, and felt relaxed and welcome, and I always felt this helped with playing well. I left class with Espirro refusing payment, and looking forward to not just training with, but also watching these students again, and the weekend roda gave me that chance.

Before then, I wanted to visit some of Fortaleza's nearby unpolluted beaches, and train some of the movements I had seen whilst here. Iguape was my first stop, and the beach continued for miles. I saw only three other people as I trained my, still rather basic, flips. The next day was Lagoinha, which was a beautiful sight. The surrounding cliffs were covered in greenery, and the white sand was perfect for training. No wonder the Capoeristas in this area were so acrobatic.

I had reserved a flight back to Rio from the city of Recife, and though I was enjoying Fortaleza, I still wanted to visit Natal, so I decided to leave after Espirro's Saturday roda. Though twenty students had taken his lessons in the week, the roda attracted many more, and after the usual one hour Brazilian wait from the arranged starting time, a group of fifty people formed the circle. I received a pleasant round of applause after an introduction from Espirro, and the Berimbaus begun. I had arrived expecting similar games to Espirro's lessons, but was to be quickly surprised.

Most of the students who had come to the roda were wearing their cleanest whites, together with their cords. One stuck out, however. I named him Dirty Guy, as he was wearing the dirtiest white trousers, with a cord that was too long, and looked like he could do with a wash. He bought a game with a Contra-Mestre Toni, and obviously wanted a hard game. As he entered under Toni's armada kick, the two became tied together in a knot resembling two tired boxers, but as they separated, Dirty Guy gave a headbutt to Toni's face. Toni's self-control surprised me, but as they returned to the foot of Espirro's berimbau, I don't think I was the only one who knew what would happen next. They cartwheeled back into the game, and then BANG. Toni gave a fast Martello straight to Dirty Guy's face, but it wasn't quick enough as he charged in on Toni and took him to the floor in a Jiu Jitsu style lock. Punches were flying, as the two players fell outside the roda, which was quickly stopped by Espirro. He then gave a five-minute talk on how to enter into an opponent and used Toni as his guinea pig, as he fired the two fastest Martellos I had ever seen before, grabbing Toni by the legs. "Isso" (that's it), nodded the student in front of me as we watched on.

Toni and Dirty Guy returned to the berimbau again, and somewhat unsurprisingly given their adrenaline pumped state, hadn't taken on board the advice just given. They entered the roda, and faced each other boxing style, with no ginga to be seen. Two misfired punches by Dirty Guy, and they were on the floor again, and this time a good ten feet outside the roda. Espirro rolled his eyes, shook his head and waved his hand for the next two players to start.

The roda continued with some games of high quality, and the students I had met in the week were showing they could play hard, as well as beautifully. A new character was soon to enter the show though. I had never seen someone with such a continuous look of smugness on them as this tall instructor who had approached the berimbau. He held his topless torso, and touched his hair in a manner that resembled the most egotistical model, and soon bought Dirty Guy's next game. Dirty Guy rose to the inevitable challenge, but his small stature was soon thrown on the floor by the much taller and stronger Ego boy (as I quickly named him). I then saw the smuggest look I will undoubtedly ever see, before reminding myself once again never to pick on someone who had many friends watching a roda.

    The roda went on for two hours with excellent energy, but the last half an hour was an experience of its own. Ego boy had risen in my estimation by inviting me to play, but not even Peixinho's rodas had prepared me to play in the final games. The more experienced students encouraged the players more and more as they landed their martellos and bencãos with force. Laughter would then fill the roda as someone executed a Vigitiva, and Espirro would jump up and down with excitement. The most enjoyable game was between two of the students I had met in the week. The less experienced one managed to land a nice Martello as his opponent, him of hand spinning fame, landed out of a flip, and it was greeted with more howls of laughter. The response, however was perfect. The player's experience and extra technique showed as he threw himself at his opponent, wrapped his legs round his body, and executed a perfectly controlled tesoura. His opponent hit the ground like a feather, and hugged his friend in a show of appreciation for the skill.

    As the roda ended to the usual hugs and kisses, I thanked Espirro, but I don't think he had realised how he, and his students, had made me see another side to Capoeira, another way to play, and express yourself. I left for my nine-hour coach journey to Natal in a daze, as if I had light bulbs glowing above my head. I had heard people talk about journeys in Capoeira, and even then, I think I realised I had just had a pretty big week in mine.

Natal is a pleasant city which, rather like Fortaleza, is surrounded by beaches. The city beaches are also relatively clean, and thus I quickly established a routine of training on these in the morning before going to Mestre Irani's academy in the evening. Again, I found someone in an Irani T-shirt who gave me directions, but unfortunately the Mestre was in England teaching when I arrived for my short time there. His group is also under Cordão de Ouro, and I again found them friendly and welcoming. The lessons under Instructor Luiz were helpful, in my games with him I was sensing some change in my ginga, which was maybe losing some of its stiffness.

I had a flight to catch, however, and I wanted to spend two days in Recife admiring its, and nearby Olinda's, churches. After another bus journey, my body began impersonating Medusa after his milk incident, but I forced my way round the stunning city. Olinda was unforgiving for someone unwell, with its steep hills and cobbled streets, but at each corner was a church slightly older and more stunning than the last and this forced my body to continue. After a small juice in a bar, I could hear my hotel bed calling me, but I had one last church to see. My guidebook claimed the church of San Francisco was the most beautiful in the city and my curiosity pushed me to know more.

The outside is certainly nothing to photograph. The outer walls were decrepit and had obviously been left untouched for several years, maybe even centuries, but the inside was like something from another world. The intricacies of the designs on the walls and ceiling, along with the amount of gold used so tastefully gave a sight to behold. It was the most stunning church I had ever seen. I was, however close to collapsing as I walked out and called on the first taxi to return me to my hotel. It was an unfortunate way to end my trip, which had given me so much. I had seen some of Brazil, but equally importantly to me, I had seen different Capoeira, and had learnt more from watching than actually training. I was heading back to Rio with some new ideas, and couldn't wait for morning training the next week. I had a ginga to work on, as well as a new direction for my game and where I wanted it to go.

Chapter Nine

Me leva Morena me leva, Me leva pra seu bangalo
(Take me brunette, take me to your bungalow...Mestre Toni)

Rio felt like home in more ways than one as I had now become so accustomed to many things. Gato and his always welcoming family, the ongoing button football championship, 'real' matches at the Maracanã, suicidal bus drivers and even the gunshots of Fallet had all become part of the routine of Rio. Training was crucial to this also, though. By training with one group, and a small selection of teachers, it is like following a particular path and the sequences trained are all designed to develop your Capoeira in a certain way. As much as I had enjoyed training with the Cordão de Ouro group, there was a big part of me that was missing my daily Senzala training, and it felt great to be back at the Leme academy. After my travels, I felt slightly wiser about Capoeira, and I was fascinated in trying to compare the games in Peixinho's roda to the ones I had seen elsewhere.

Ramos continued to work his students hard in his lessons, and his music classes were certainly beginning to have an effect as I felt my berimbau playing improving with each week. Gato's morning lessons were as before, with all of us working our basics over and over. However, I had made a conscious decision to work on my ginga, and each morning I was spending twenty minutes moving around a chair whilst making a distinct effort to follow the rhythm. This is something that Gato still criticised about me, and now I was learning more and more the importance of the ginga, I was determined to improve mine.

I was also beginning to train more with Mestre Toni, and the friendly atmosphere within his group, allied to my improving Portuguese, was making his group feel more like where I belonged. His rodas weren't nearly as intimidating as Peixinho's, and I felt more relaxed as I tried to incorporate more of what I was learning. I had picked up a kick used from the floor called Chapeu de Couro from his group, and was beginning to use this more in the roda, seeing the moments when I could place it correctly.

Unfortunately for many of the current group of gringos, who were often making up a third of a class, it was time to move on. Medusa left shortly after I returned to Rio, and his dry humour and wit was to be missed. The girls had a mixed trip in Recife, with Brie's Mestre alienating Michelle and Ruchi and often not allowing them to play in their rodas due to them being from a different group. Brie herself, though a member of the group in Canada, had had to be known under a different nickname whilst she was there. They had also felt strangled by the rules this Mestre gave them. They had to be in at certain times at night, and it seemed like a school camp to me. They were relieved to return to Rio, but for Brie and Michelle it was time to leave. Brie left for Canada, and Michelle back to New Zealand.

There were new arrivals however. Camarão (shrimp) was just 18 years old, but had already trained for nine years in Copenhagen, under a student of Peixinho's, Professor Steen. Dion had also arrived, from Edinburgh. He had helped develop the group in Scotland, and had stayed with Gato for several months just two years before. He was now working with a television company in America, aiming to gain some ideas for a program on Capoeira.

Camarão's bright red hair and light features helped him to look even less Brazilian than myself, and being a student of Peixinho's he decided to move into the house straight away. Though he had considerably less talent in the kitchen than the girls, his specialty being jam rolls, his talent in Capoeira was undeniable. He had reached the instructor's cord of grey, and soon received his blue, but it was with music that he most excelled. He had been playing percussion since his childhood, and was more than happy leading Peixinho's rodas singing whilst on berimbau, atabaque or tambourine. His confidence defied his age and I was spending my afternoons learning from him. I finally hit the atabaque correctly, and learnt numerous songs from him. Dion was another who loved to play berimbau, and soon joined us by the pool.

This was good timing. Outside of my ginga practice, I had decided to listen to Capoeira music as much as possible and understand the rhythms more. The next step was logically to play more music, and learn more of the songs. I first wanted to learn more of the popular songs that were used regularly in the rodas I was playing in. Each group has its favourite songs, and Senzala was no different, using many of Mestre Toni's. I had found the Cordão de Ouro groups I had met used many of Mestre Suassuna's songs, and I soon found some of his CDs to listen to. This was to take up much more of my time in my remaining months.

One thing I hadn't missed about Rio whilst I had been traveling was its dangers. Though living in Fallet undoubtedly carried its own worries, the streets of Rio provide many dangers of their own. Up until now I had been fortunate. I had had a credit card taken from my wallet on Ipanema beach, but I had never been threatened or had anything of worth stolen. However, my luck was about to run out.

Rio is infamous for its dangers, particularly for tourists, and these can often be exaggerated by guidebooks. They do exist though, and even Cariocas never drive without their doors locked in case of car jackings. Camarão had found trouble in his first week when he was beaten by three youths on a bus, and it was whilst waiting for a bus that I became a victim.

It was early afternoon, and the sun was blisteringly hot, as I traveled to Ramos' class. The bus was late and I placed my bag on the floor, something I rarely did, as just two minutes later, a guy of about seventeen had grabbed it and was running down the street. I instinctively gave chase, and we both ran at half pace on Santa Teresa's cobbled streets in our flip-flops. I started to wonder what I would do if I caught him, would my training take over? In truth I had no idea, and never got to decide anyhow. He ran up one of the many steep hills available to him, and after two minutes we were both exhausted. I couldn't help thinking it must be amusing for onlookers to watch a chase scene where both people involved are walking, as that was what we were now doing. I hid behind a car, as he turned to see if I had made any ground. As he walked up the hill, I had recovered my breath and started to give chase again, but it was to no avail as a motorbike sped past and picked him up.

Some nearby residents quickly provided me with a juice and a lift to the police station, but these cases are rarely solved. I was more worried about missing the class in truth, as my insurance would cover my lost belongings. However, I finally had my Rio mugging story to tell, but only had to wait two more weeks before I had a far more exciting one.

With the festive season almost upon Brazil, classes were about to take a break, but there was time for one more celebration. Peixinho's birthday is just before Christmas, and it is now almost tradition that he is given a 'surprise' party. This consisted of a large roda on the Friday evening, which gave rise to the best energy I had ever known with Senzala. Many of Peixinho's students had come, and there were some fine games amongst Mestres Beto, Feijão and Toni. Peixinho then got to play Gato, in what must provoke huge memories amongst them, to great applause, followed by some Makulele with Toni at the atabaque. I had heard some brilliant Makulele at Suassuna's academy, but I never thought anyone could match Toni, and the power of his voice, when providing the energy for this dance.

Gato, and a percussion class given by Contra Mestre Arruda filled the following day. I was always highly impressed by Arruda. I had been to his batizado near Niteroi earlier in the year, and he had proved friendly, welcoming and able to give a roda a lift with his presence. His music was excellent, and Camarão was particularly excited with his presence at the event.

The evening was devoted to a music competition. Many students of Senzala had written songs for the prize of a Peixinho berimbau, and were judged by Gato and an old friend of his, Mestre Leopoldinha. The standard was high, and brought a mixture of fast catchy lyrics together with Ladainhas (stories sung at the beginning of rodas). The winner was Professor Pulmão (lung), whose powerful voice was such an asset for him. He celebrated at the night's party where to Camarão's tambourine he rapped with Mestre Toni, in what was a fitting end to the celebrations.

There was time for one more training session before the presents were opened. I was still training in the mornings, and Gato had decided to invite two visiting American students to join us by the pool. The three of us were working hard, doing Meu Lua de Compasso, and then dodging our partners, before giving another one. After an hour, the heat meant my trousers were soaked through, but Gato had more planned, and we were then countering each other's Armadas with rasteiras, and getting to our feet quickly to repeat the sequence. As Gato went to start cleaning the pool, the Americans assumed the lesson was over and began to pack their things together. However, I had seen the glint that Gato had in his eye before, and knew he was going to insist on some more, and it was just a minute later when he said "how about this. Give a bencão, and I give a rasteira." Twenty minutes later, even I was surprised as we were still training, practicing a Meu Lua de Compasso in a headstand, before we finally called it a day.

I thanked God for my now high level of fitness, but I think Gato's visitors were slightly shocked, and left looking in serious need of a rest. I later managed to interrupt Gato's work, and ask him about the lesson, and he simply smiled and said, "Yeah, we really killed them ah?" I couldn't help but chuckle as I replied, "oh yes, we certainly did."

Christmas in Brazil isn't nearly as celebrated as in England, and even my local church was only half full on the big day. I was lucky enough to spend my time at Gato and Beatrice's families, and couldn't believe that the looks in the family extended all the way to the nieces too. As I ate another piece of chocolate cake, I couldn't help thinking that there were some seriously good genes being passed in this part of Rio.

As classes stopped for the holiday period, I contented myself with more sessions on my ginga by the pool, followed by some more championship games of Button Football. After my early successes, Gabriel was making good progress. His yellow and blue midfielder was scoring freely, and not even my Fluminense forward could halt a series of defeats for me. Fortunately, Gabriel was traveling with Suassuna to help organise the upcoming Capoeirando, a Senzala/Cordão de Ouro event in Bahia, and I was to be given a chance to reorganise my team, as well as train without his distracting ways.

There was one more celebration to be had however, before classes resumed in the New Year. I had always admired

Rio's celebrations to welcome in the New Year, and with London continuously disappointing in its plans, I was high with expectation. Dion's Spanish girlfriend, Illisia, had arrived and Ruchi had returned from her extended trip to the Amazon, so with Camarão too, the five of us set out for Copacabana beach. Mario had actually warned us not to be outside and near the house at midnight due to the amount of guns which were fired, but we had no intention of returning until late. After the traditional fireworks, a series of concerts were planned along all of Rio's beaches, and large stages had been erected through the week in preparation.

I was still fresh from my recent robbery, and Camarão certainly had some mental scars from his assault, and thus we were always aware of our surroundings. I had walked the route from Santa Teresa to Gloria many times without incident, but this night we weren't so lucky. Dion had taken some video footage of a very old looking tree, as we continued down the road. Soon after, we were stopped. There were four youths in total, though only two approached us. One was wearing a Flamengo football shirt, and it was him that pulled out a revolver. I had seen guns before, and recently I had walked passed a bandit in my road that was carrying one, so there was no shock factor. Brie and I had once left the house early one morning when she whispered to me "don't look down the road." Of course I quickly turned and looked down the road to see three bandits carrying Uzis.

Dion was first in line and I had seen him pack his camera into the bun bag he was carrying. The robber was becoming edgy as Dion fumbled with his wallet, and banged the gun into Dion's face, bruising his eye instantly. He quickly handed over the wallet, and began to walk off. However, as quickly as I could say to myself "you jammy so and so", the other robber noticed the bag around his waist and the production company's camera was gone.

Illisia, who was now crying uncontrollably, was next in line and she handed over her camera and wallet before hugging to Dion's side. As she did though, I caught Ruchi in the corner of my eye walking past ignoring everything. As I was talking with her I had to make the choice, to go or not to go. Ruchi's dark skin often disguised her foreign roots, where as with my blonde hair I always felt like I was noticed, and this crossed my mind. I also knew that my wallet was worth more than its twenty reais contents, and was certainly not worth the risk of getting shot for. I let Ruchi go, and threw my wallet on the floor.

Camarão was having trouble, however. The gun holding bandit was becoming wild with panic, and swung the gun at the back of Camarão's head as he struggled to pass over his mobile phone. The other bandit picked up my wallet as his friends in the background began to shout "Mata los, mata los" (kill them, kill them) and so when it was my turn, I thought I may be in trouble. He waved his gun in my face shouting "dinheiro, dinheiro" (money, money!), whilst I pointed at his friend saying "ele tem, ele tem" (he has it, he has it), but he wasn't listening and he pointed the gun to my face. There were no images of my life passing in front of my eyes like in the films, just a gun, but relief soon came as his friend pulled his shirt and they ran off down the street. Well, I guess they didn't want to miss the fireworks.

They had certainly hit the jackpot. A top of the range video camera, two cameras, a mobile phone and four wallets was the reward for not getting caught. Ruchi may have escaped the robbers, but was now the only one with any money, and thus she had to pay for the rest of our night, which was certainly enjoyable after the initial period of recuperation. Illicia was particularly scared and upset, and Dion controlled his obvious fury well whilst he consoled her. Camarão couldn't believe his luck after his bus incident just weeks before, but was maturing fast in his new dangerous environment, and the incident helped him with this.

Camarão and I talked about our training after this. Camarão and Dion were the most experienced Capoeiristas amongst us, and I would have backed them to take the robbers down if it weren't for the gun, which whether fake or not, had the desired effect. However, to risk not just your own life, but also the whole group's, in an act of heroism would have been somewhat unnecessary, and I am glad no one risked the temptation to try a Martello. After all, a mobile phone is easily replaced.

The fireworks were the most spectacular I had ever seen, but didn't impress the million Brazilians who were on the beaches. Though they cheered each one, this was the first year they had been fired from boats offshore as opposed to from the beaches, and apparently it ruined the effect of feeling the firework was falling on top of the people. This was actually exactly what the authorities had hoped, as the number of injuries from the fireworks falling on the packed beaches was growing each year. It certainly beat London for an eventful New Year.

Shortly after New Year, classes returned and the Rio training routine continued. The forthcoming Capoeirando event was to have a big impact, however. It was to be held in Ilheus, about seven hours drive south of Bahia's capital, Salvador, and Ruchi, Dion and Illisia all traveled early to visit Salvador before its start. Gato had organized the event along with Suassuna, and wanted to finish a project he was working on before he traveled; therefore early morning training was off for the time being. I told our newest arrival, Tom Thumb, how lucky he was not to be getting up at 7am everyday.

Tom was a further member of Pedro's group, and we soon realized we had two things in common. Firstly, Tom's bright red hair and white skin would make him look as unbrazilian as myself, and secondly, he also struggled with

Martello. It was a close call as to who had the worst Martello, so I settled for the fact that neither of us could do it. Tom's problem was also the stiffness in his hips, and, like me, he struggled with flexibility in general.

We started to train without Gato, and Tom was enjoying the classes, especially Toni's, who he had met before in Scotland. However, Tom was struggling to come to terms with my obsession with pad training. He argued that by doing the techniques with a partner helped prepare you for the game itself, and he had a point. However, endless kicking of a pad has its own benefits. It allows you to feel a technique, and find your balance, which sometimes you can't do when you're concentrating on performing a sequence with a partner. It also helps with learning to gauge the distance concerned with each kick, and improve its speed, but most of all, I found it great fun. The clapping sound the pad made when it was hit well had turned into a joy for me, and previously, Rob and I had created a game of attempting to kick the pad hard enough to send it into the pool. You couldn't do that with a partner. Well not if you liked him anyhow!

Tom, like myself, needed to work on his basic kicks, but had decided to come now so he could attend the Capoeirando event. The day before we were to leave, another gringo joined us, Jim, who was soon to be christened Cascão (crusty). Jim was tall, slim and in his late twenties, and was someone who clearly enjoyed travelling light, as his only luggage was a small record bag which held some extra underwear and Capoeira trousers. He had been taking lessons from Medusa in Norwich, and it showed. Jim could backflip, somersault and bend his naturally elastic body in a variety of ways. However, he couldn't dodge a kick if his life depended on it, and was in Brazil to "work on his basics". He also had an ambition to Folhaseca before he left Brazil. This acrobatic move requires a player to kick his leg straight up in the air, and then allow his body to follow through an entire 360-degree flip. It requires no fear, and Cascão certainly had this attribute. However, it was his basics that were about to be worked as we left for Ilheus, and what was soon to be christened 'Capoeira Bootcamp'.

Chapter Ten

Vou me embora pra Bahia, Eu aqui nao fico nao
(I am going to Bahia, I'm not staying here...Popular)

Traveling through the North East using the national bus system, I had developed ways of making the journeys as comfortable as possible. Essentials were as follows:

- Walkman and tapes (at least five depending on journey's length)
- Spare batteries
- Biscuits
- Water
- Jumper to combat air conditioning
- Brazil guide book

With reading making me travel sick, small sections of a guide book were all I could handle, and of my tapes, I would always include my Springsteen Live, which would make ninety minutes fly by as I imagined I was in that New York crowd. I had tried other sugary foods than biscuits, but found them to make me feel sick, and the time on earlier journeys, had quickly taught me that the air conditioning would always be on maximum, so a jumper became essential. Though it would always annoy the person sitting next to me that it took me five minutes to position everything correctly before sitting, I always found that if I followed my rules, the journey would fly by.

Something that did always amuse me was watching where people left the bus. I saw men with briefcases and suits being left in the middle of fields, and this always left me with images of them trying to sell insurance to the thin cows that lived there. However, I guess all towns, not matter how small, need some business visitors.

The journey to Ilheus would take twenty-two hours, and the jumper I had packed was to be highly unnecessary, as the coach was not air-conditioned. The powerful Brazilian sun beat down as we left Rio, prepared to sweat for the next day. I sat next to Jim, and the first couple of hours flew by as we told each other our full repertoire of jokes, before getting to know each other. Tom wasn't so lucky. He was sitting next to Ia, a recent arrival from Denmark who had arranged to meet her Danish teacher and group at the event, but decided to visit Rio first. Though only twenty, Ia was a headstrong girl, who didn't suffer fools gladly. In fact, her temper could be quite fierce, and was set off relatively easily. When this was added to the fact that she was a natural worrier, as well as asking questions constantly, Tom's journey was to feel slightly more than twenty-two hours.

As Jim and I caught some sleep overnight, we were alerted to Ia's temper. "Shut up, shut the fuck up!" she was telling the couple in the seats in front of her as they chattered away, but knowing they couldn't understand her. "Man, who fuckin' talks at 5:00 in the morning, ah? Tell me that? Fuckin hell." I caught Tom's face showing a mixture of a smile and a look of embarrassment as he attempted to calm Ia down. Jim simply turned to me, told me how excited he was for the fiftieth time, and then went back to sleep.

As if the journey wasn't long enough, and Ia's fuse short enough already, it was ended with a two-hour taxi journey. Our hotel was only 12km from the Bus station, but our taxi driver drove round each hotel in the area until he finally found one with some Capoeiristas. I had never been so relieved to see Gato in all my life. He gave our driver some instructions for our hotel and we set off again. Fortunately, on the way we found the Danish group, headed by their teacher Steen and Camarão, who had been given a lift by Peixinho (it took them just 15 hours!). Ia screamed "let me out, let me out!" as she jumped over Tom in the back seat to join her group. He let out a mighty sigh of relief.

Though it took our taxi driver another 30 minutes to find our hotel, it was actually only a ten-minute walk along the beach from the rest. We were sharing with some Americans who had come from California for the event, and some more Brazilians. The other hotels based all those who had chosen to camp, as well as all the teachers who had come. The list was an impressive line-up. The next four days were to see classes from Mestres Gato, Peixinho, Ramos, Suassuna, Deputado, Onça, Jogo de Dentro, Lobão and Acordeon. Also present were many other teachers and Mestres who had traveled to the event, which was jointly hosted by Cordão de Ouro and Senzala. As we went to the opening party, I described to Jim some of the faces I recognized. Kibe and his friends from São Paulo had arrived, Virgulinho was a student of Mestre Irani in Natal, and I finally met Irani too. Unfortunately, my hopes of Mestre Espirro coming were dashed, but an exciting energy existed as almost inevitably, a roda was formed and the games started.

    We had arrived a day before lessons were to begin, but with good reason. Our hotel was separated from the main complex by a ten-minute walk on the beach, but the beach itself went on for many more miles. The sand was as white as I had ever seen, and only a slightly darkened sky ruined the setting. After playing some games on the beach, my first with Jim, we met with Gato, Beatrice and Gabriel, who was looking decidedly cool, or at least trying to, in his rasta gear. Where he did actually look cooler was when he executed a perfectly timed Rastiera do chão on Suassuna's son, who came crashing down. Mestre Deputado, who is another student of Mestre Bimba, was leading the roda. He was being shown enormous respect by the Cordão de Ouro players who formed the majority of the roda. Kibe and co were inevitably at the forefront, and their play was already beginning to cause quite a stir amongst any visitors, particularly the Americans, many of whom had never seen such a gathering of good Capoeiristas.

The games were of a high quality, and the energy fantastic as everyone was obviously enjoying the setting. Many players were even playing in their Speedos, as they came from the sea or beach to take part in the roda. With a large queue forming to play, I was happy to save myself for the coming day's training. After a talk from Suassuna on the training we could expect, the day ended, as most were to, with a roda, a party and some samba de roda.

The talk at the breakfast table the next morning was all of groups, teachers and who was going to train with whom. The classes were divided into beginners, two intermediate and an advanced lesson, and then end with rodas, leaving the afternoon for relaxing. My first class was an intermediate lesson with Deputado and Onça, who are former students of Bimba. In a good-humoured class they showed lots of movements not often seen in a roda. These included grabs and elbow strikes to the head, and certainly showed the nastier side to Capoeira.

I then joined Jim in the beginner's class, which was taken by Mestre Jogo de Dentro, an Angoleiran master who was a student of Mestre João Pequeno, who in turn had learnt from the legendary Mestre Pastinha. He worked on a basic sequence involving a Meu Lua de Compasso, and then an exit in negativa. Jim remarked on my relaxed way of doing the sequence, but he had obviously not seen me in a roda yet. He didn't get the chance in the afternoon roda either, which was again with a huge queue of people, and again Suassuna's students were dominating proceedings. Their style of moving through a bridge before kicking, and then jumping, was starting to inspire other students, and people began incorporating them into their games. By the end of the week, this was to have become slightly ridiculous as every game was incorporating these movements, making them slightly predictable.

The afternoon saw more rodas take place, and then the inevitable party. The parties were bringing a real atmosphere to the meeting, and guaranteeing that all the games were between friends. I think this also had to do with the meeting being organised by just two groups. Much of the violence I had seen in Capoeira had come from people from opposing groups, but this meeting was appearing to avoid it, and I didn't see one roda spill over into violence.

I deliberately avoided the main intermediate class the next day, and headed for the smaller lesson to be given by

Mestre Lobão, who is from São Paulo. He gave an excellent class showing various ways of escaping an attempted Vigitiva, and then some counter attacks. My particular favourite was stepping away from your opponent as he tried to give a Vigitiva throw and felling him with a tesoura. When done correctly, it was very impressive.

The second class saw Suassuna and his crew of students demonstrating some of the sequences that were becoming more popular in the rodas as the week progressed. With so many people wanting to take part in the class, the area was soon full of people attempting movements with queda da rins and bridges. In fact, the class was so popular once you entered a bridge, there often wasn't enough space to come out again. After twenty minutes, I gave up and managed to find some space in a separate room to practice some movements alone. It was a shame to miss Suassuna's class, but with so much happening at once, there wasn't a great deal of time to think about it.

With the daytime and evening rodas giving few chances for playing, the Brazilians idea of a Hotel Roda was greeted warmly. The American/English/Brazilian mix led to some interesting accents in the singing, but guaranteed good energy as everyone took the chance to play. The smaller roda also gave the chance for people to try a few songs and was one of the few times I led the singing in Brazil. This was something I was always highly self-concious of. Camarao was proof that gringos could sing just as well as Brazilians in a roda, but I lacked confidence in my pronunciation, voice and timing to lead the singing in rodas, though practicing with Camarao had certainly helped.

After a rest and another evening floodlit roda, the usual party took over. Cervejas were cracked open and the Brazilians led the way with the samba. As was typical with Samba de Rodas, many of the songs were created there and then, and were mixed in with more traditional songs. The American girls were more forthcoming than the men, but the English tended to stick with their conservative ways and just watch. However, one American was especially keen. Jason had traveled from New York for the event and certainly had the American 'Up and at em' attitude. He was always near the front of queues for the rodas, and equally samba held no fear for him. Despite not having too much idea of the dance, he jumped in at every opportunity and always with a large smile. His attitude epitomised the feel good factor that was becoming prominent as the event continued.

After two days of changeable weather, the event's third day finally saw sunshine. It also saw the arrival of Mestre Acordeon. Acordeon was a student of Mestre Bimba and has become famous within Capoeira for his play, his knowledge, his work in the US and his music. He was amongst the first Brazilians to start an academy in the US, and in more recent years his CDs have become amongst the most popular and recognisable Capoeira music.

When he arrived at the beginning of the classes, it was as if a celebrity had entered the building. People were clambering for photos, or at least a handshake, as he tried to enjoy his welcome to the meeting. I was doing some stretching exercises with Tom, but was becoming increasingly excited over Acordeon's class. I had been lucky enough to visit his academy in San Francisco whilst on holiday a year previously and had enjoyed his energy and approach. However, his entrance had attracted a lot of attention and already the class was becoming as full as Suassuna's the previous day.

My worries were unnecessary however, as Acordeon gave most of his class as a talk with few movements. He spoke in English and in Portuguese of the importance of rhythm in the roda, and used an atabaque and Mestre Irani to demonstrate his points. It was an important lesson for a Capoeirista lacking in rhythm, and I still had his words of "The Englishman needs to work on his ginga" in my head from when I had visited him in San Francisco the year before. In fact, these words ran through my mind each time I passed twenty minutes by the pool practicing my ginga with a chair. I took his lesson in like an enthusiastic schoolboy learning to read. I was also determined to take any more sessions Acordeon was to give at the event.

Gato took the second intermediate class. If I was a fish out of the water for Acordeon's lesson, I quickly dived back in for Gato's as he showed many of the movements I knew so well from my hours by his pool. After the class, he made three rodas, giving everyone a chance to play, and I was determined to take it.

At moments throughout my games in Brazil, I felt something in my body click, and my training kicking in. Suddenly, it would all seem easier and it was like my opponent's movements were becoming slower. This was certainly one of those times, and as I played against fellow yellow and orange cords, I began to feel confident enough to enter underneath kicks, try Vigitivas and Rasteras and let my kicks go a little faster. It certainly helped that Ramos's advanced class was still in progress, so the rodas were yet to be filled with the fast kicking, high jumping Brazilians. I saw many Americans also taking the opportunity to play and the energy began to grow steadily as more people joined in. One girl got so excited after one game, she kissed me to release some emotion. It made me realise that Capoeira really could have strange effects on people!

I was happy to sit back and watch as the advanced students began joining the rodas. I had had my games, and though my body was exhausted, the roda's energy, and my happiness with my games, gave me a huge smile. My training was working, and I was enjoying every minute of it.

The evening roda was notable for one particular game. Ramos had been dominating the roda, playing anyone that wanted to play, and was clearly enjoying testing his game against the various professors. It was proving quite a spectacle until a screech of pain from Ramos saw him running out the roda holding his shoulder. It was dislocated, and though the roda continued, the energy fell considerably.

That was of course only until the samba rhythms were beating away again and the Festa was started. As the different groups mixed more in the classes, the evening parties became even noisier and more social. Gabriel was still attempting to look good in a Rasta hat, but his girlfriend for the week obviously didn't mind.

Jim was using a different technique to attract the ladies. He had befriended Miguel, a small, tanned Portuguese character who seemed to have a distinct way with women. He had soon become Jim's interpreter, however, this was usually ending up with Miguel opening a conversation, introducing Jim, and then having his way. This left Jim with some rather awkward silences to fill. Miguel's 'success rate' was growing rapidly and even the fiery Ia didn't repel his obsessive ways. It seemed we had met a true life Casanova, but Miguel had much more to show yet.

Jim's luck seemed down and he convinced me of this when his described his morning training. In an Angola class with Mestre Jogo de Dentro, he had been shown a sequence including a chamada. This is a movement where one Capoeirista stops and lifts his arms, breaking the game, before his opponent joins him, and then continues. Jim's Danish partner had worried him slightly when she requested "I want to be the tree, let me be the tree!" before doing the movement, but then left Jim aghast when she later stormed out the class crying "You're not very nice, I just can't do this anymore!!" Jim's dry humour was to become a constant highlight for us, and his partnership with Miguel was only just beginning.

The final day of the event was to see just one longer session given by a Mestre to each group. I decided to join the smaller intermediate group and couldn't believe my luck as Mestre Acordeon stepped up to give the class. Once again he spoke of the importance of rhythm within Capoeira and using the atabaque, he made the class do esquivas to his beat. He then taught a sequence involving moving underneath an armada kick, before felling the kicker with a tesoura. The small number of people meant he corrected each pairing, as Beatrice filmed all.

He then stopped the class to give a further talk on the importance of music in Capoeira. The man was certainly an impressive teacher, and his large frame and grey beard didn't manage to hide a welcoming smile that helped relax his students as he talked in a clear and softly spoken manner. The man had an aura of greatness, and I felt highly fortunate to be listening to him and his teachings. As a few advanced students joined the group, he had the class kicking Meu Lua de Compassos down the hall, but always to his rhythm.

As the lesson finished, I quickly found Jim practicing a sequence that Peixinho had shown in his class. He insisted on not leaving until he knew the sequence by heart and we practiced together. He then became like an excited six year old at Christmas as I told him that there were plenty more sequences like this to come in Rio. As I thought of Jim's enthusiasm, I couldn't get Acordeon's lesson from my head. I had felt like I had learnt so much in just ninety minutes, and would practice this lesson many more times by the pool. Surely one of the best lessons I would ever take.

As Jim and I walked back to the hotel together, we were once again greeted with another Hotel Roda. It had been started once again by the Brazilians and Miguel was singing away as Jim and I began playing. A Brazilian Professor from Minas Gerais soon bought my game, and I felt like I was playing well. Maybe too well it seemed, as the professor over-estimated my level and gave a very quick Meu Lua de Compasso. I almost froze as his foot passed just millimetres from my face. I had no time to esquiva or move to the floor. He held nothing back on the kick, and I was left with only God knowing how my shoulders and head were still connected. There was nothing quite like a playing a Brazilian to keep one's feet on the ground.

Though the event's parties had proved as popular as the classes, the final night gave a chance to experience another part of Brazilian culture, Carnival. The town of Itabuma was less then an hour's drive from Ilheus and Mestre Cigarro organised a coach to transport some of his American students to the event. Myself, Tom, Jim and Miguel were invited along too by the ever friendly Jason. Some Brazilians also joined in, and with Cigarro concerned over the dangers of Carnival for some gringos, they were to become chaperones for the night.

Sensing plenty of opportunities, Miguel was soon away from the group trying his luck with his trusty sidekick Jim. Tom and I stuck with Jason, who was as keen as ever to dance, and some of his American friends. The streets were crammed with people dancing to the enormous floats that passed, and the mixture of colours was encapsulating. Each float was packed with women in luminous green, or yellow, or orange bikinis. The men wore bright T-shirts, and each float was decorated to add to the atmosphere. The evening was a great success, though the high numbers of police proved that there were potential security issues, as I was later to find out. All the groups met back at the coach at 4am, though it proved that Miguel had had more success than Jim as he returned without his translator.

The rather enormous frame of Cigarro also appeared, but unfortunately only to explain that the coach wouldn't start.

After twenty minutes of watching more floats finish their circuit, Tom, Jason, Jim and all boarded the still stationary coach. I decided to quench my thirst and soon found a nearby drinks seller. Fortunately, when I returned the coach no longer had a problem. Unfortunately, I only knew this because it was nowhere to be seen. I faced my reality. I was a fair skinned, blond gringo, in the middle of an ever-maddening carnival, surrounded by drunken Brazilians and riot police (who I think were sober). I estimated a taxi at fifty reais, and I had fourteen. It was 4:30 am.

With my improving Portuguese, I became slightly nervous to learn that the bus station was too dangerous at this time, and that the first bus would leave around 6 O'clock. After finding a hotel owner who found me rather amusing (the amount of Brazilians who find gringos funny can be quite unnerving at times) and so let me use his toilet, I decided to walk into the main section of the Carnival and try and enjoy the spectacle. However, being alone I was becoming far more aware of how many people were staring at me. In Rio, a gringo is commonplace, but the small town of Itabuma is different. I guarded my fourteen Reais like my life depended on it, knowing I would be left stranded if a pickpocket took his chance.

The Carnival was split into two roads, one with floats going out, and one with them returning. The sides were covered with drink sellers, and in between were groups of

Police, standing in sixes looking for trouble. This wasn't proving too difficult to find as drunkeness began to progress into outright fighting. This was proving relatively easy to avoid, but the Police reaction was more difficult. Instead of picking out the guilty parties, the clearly pre-planned reaction was to swing their batons recklessly, hitting anyone in their path, and hope this stopped any fight. My heart was pumping faster then in any roda from the previous week as I received a baton on my back. I rushed through the crowds, with any hint of drunkenness in the distant past, trying to find a place to rest and catch my breath.

As it was, it proved difficult to find a place without a fight taking place, or being 'stopped' by the police. As I looked around though, all those not involved in being beaten or giving a beating, were actually acting quite normally, drinking and dancing. This was carnival. A mixture of sound, colour, dancing, drinking and 'socialising'. I decided that if I wasn't to spend the next hours practicing my esquivas, I needed to relax. I bought a beer and decided to 'practice my Portuguese', as a Danish friend of mine once termed chatting up women. I soon met a lovely girl called Christina, who helped take my mind off any potential beatings, before showing me to the bus station.

I finally arrived back to my hotel bed at 9am to find Jim, Tom and Jason in the same state they had been in when the coach had left five-hours earlier, asleep. I soon joined them, but after just surviving one night, was still puzzled as to how Brazilians party at Carnival for five days!

Chapter Eleven

Nao Sou daqui, nao tenho amor, sou da Bahia, de Sao Salvador
(I'm not from here, I'm not in love, I'm from Bahia, from
Salvador...Popular)

Bahia and its people are infamous in Brazil for a relaxed life style. Baianas talk slower, walk slower and enjoy some of the best beaches in Brazil in which to play Capoeira. After the training intensity of the event, it was agreed that some days relaxing on a beach were well deserved so Miguel, Jim, Tom and myself settled in for the two-hour bus ride to Itacare, the surfing capital of Bahia.

The town is typical of some of the beach towns of Brazil that are becoming increasingly popular with tourists. Streets of new restaurants, bars and hotels always lead the way to one of the town's beaches, and Itacare's were beautiful. Prices all over Brazil often rise for Gringos, so with this in mind, Miguel was sent to impersonate a Brazilian and find a hotel. It was only later that Gato told me he found it hard to believe that Miguel could hide his Portuguese accent to fool any Brazilian.

Itacare is fortunate enough to be surrounded by beaches so the lazy tourist can pick and choose at will. It is also known for its parties and Miguel already had his eye on conquering the female half of the town. After one night, his first 'victim' had succumbed. Jim had decided to join me in an early night with a view to training the next day. Even after the 'Bootcamp' training was never too far from our agenda. Jim also had big ideas for what he wanted to train.

We walked down two beaches before Jim was happy. On the sand we trained with some exercises for balance I had been shown in the Northeast just two months before. Jim had fantastic natural flexibility but his esquivas were lacking balance and definition, and with this in mind, we trained as if doing a session by Gato's pool. After this, Jim had his own agenda.

A grass verge bordered our chosen beach and now that Jim was warm, he was ready to practice what he wanted, his Mortal (a somersault). I had seen many more acrobatics in Fortaleza than in Rio, but had never thought of training in them myself. Medusa was always learning a new flip or spin and had certainly influenced Jim back in England. With my lack of flexibility and general fear of letting my body flip through the air, I had generally left the acrobatics to the kids, but they had entranced Jim. He was certainly fearless as he leapt off the verge. As always on Brazil's beaches, a boy had soon joined us and was giving Jim advice. Like most things, learning these techniques is always easier for a child who has no fear and plenty of natural flexibility.

The other movement that had Jim obsessed was the Folha Seca (dry leaf). This movement involves kicking a leg straight up before allowing the body to follow it all the way round. Miguel had taught this to Jim in Ilheus, and had him imagining he was kicking a football as hard as he could before taking off, and he was coming close. It was all very impressive for someone with only a few months Capoeira behind them, but showed how some movements are picked up more rapidly than others.

After Jim finally managed to stop practicing and I had finally convinced him that I was too chicken to try, we thought a drink was well deserved. Jim was also keen to re-unite his partnership with Miguel, which was improving his Portuguese, if nothing else.

Nightlife in Itacare started as many nights in Brazil, on the street. 'Barracas' (bars) line the street selling beer and cachaça (Brazilian rum). Also being Brazil, nobody really took to the street until midnight, and then headed for an organised Festa at about 2am. Coming from a country where most bars close at the slightly ridiculous time of 11pm, I always found this quite strange, especially as it led to many people in the clubs looking exhausted by 3am.

The time of day was the last thing on Miguel's mind, and it was difficult to attempt a conversation with him as he spent his time looking for potential conquests. We became accustomed to him stopping you in mid-flow with a "Man, look!" It would then take a second or two before you realised he hadn't listened to anything you had said, and he would follow up with his developing catchphrase, "if I don't sleep with that girl tonight, I'll die!" All slightly ridiculous, and before you could give an opinion, he was already talking with the girl and attempting to introduce Jim to the friends. Tom and I would always keep an interested eye whilst the Capoeira conversation continued.

Itacare's trance music scene and my slight lack of interest in Miguel's conquering activities led to this being my last 'night out'. I was more hopeful of finding some entertainment at the local capoeira schools, and it was entertainment I found. Mestre Jamaica ran an academy with a stunning view of a beach surrounded by fishing boats. Unfortunately, the teaching wasn't so impressive. The lesson showed some of Bahia's style of capoeira using a different negativa from which I was used to, and a generally more relaxed way compared to Rio. The roda was to show this even more. Peixinho's rodas in Rio of an organised queue for playing, buying of the game at a good time and an atmosphere of singing and clapping were like a different world compared to the roda we found ourselves in.

Players were buying games at any moment and then generally showing a few tricks before becoming bored and ending the game. I bought some games but rarely got to 'play'. My opponent was always more intent on flipping as high as possible than trying to exchange movements with me. Miguel had more luck and played well with some more experienced members of the group. However, Mestre Jamaica never had control on his roda and none of us felt a huge a amount of respect existed between him and his students.

After about twenty-five minutes, the roda was losing some of the little energy that had existed, however, I had never seen the rhythm change as it did. The next game that was bought saw the roda change to samba de roda, with all the female students joining in. Some male students then started dancing too as we all looked on slightly bemused. After another five minutes, the lead berimbau again took up the rhythm of regional and the capoeira continued. This all seemed normal to the twenty or so students who made the roda and everyone was clearly enjoying themselves. It was certainly a different way of doing things though, and was further proof of the varieties that exist in capoeira. As I was later told by Mestre Acordeon, "these things aren't wrong, just different".

After our somewhat eventful night at Jamaica's, Tom and I were beginning to find ourselves ready to visit Salvador, the Capital City of Bahia. However, we still had a final beach to visit whilst in Itacare. Through a nearby forest, via a winding footpath, lay Prainha (Little Beach). After the four of us took a wrong turning through some mud pools, the expected forty five minute walk took almost one hour thirty minutes, but it was worth the effort. The beach was a beautiful white sandy cove about half a mile long, with a bank encasing the cove with palm trees. It was free of bars and drink sellers, and made a perfect place for a final day of relaxation before arriving in the city.

Jim didn't take long to start training his acrobatics with Miguel once again, and they were even patient enough to help me with my backflip. Put politely, it needed plenty of work. Jim's Folha Seca was improving rapidly and he was clearly pleased with it. He also realised that this was his big chance to learn movements such as this whilst he had the beaches at his disposal. With this in mind, and Miguel's obvious liking for nightlife, they decided to stay in Itacare before heading to Salvador. Tom and I were ready however, and I was hopeful this would be a grand highlight of my trip.

Salvador was Brazil's first capital city and remained so for two hundred years until 1763. Its initial success was based around the sugarcane industry and thus thousands of slaves from Africa were shipped to the city in this period. Perhaps like nowhere else in the world these African roots grew stronger over the years and are now a crucial part of Bahian, and Salvadors' culture. The African religion of Candomble is still widely practiced in the city, and it was also here that capoeira was to develop.

The slaves that managed to escape from their owners formed Quilombos, which were villages where they lived freely and practiced their African culture. This not only meant Candomble, but Capoeira too. The Quilombos would often attack the slaveowners land and there are many myths surrounding great slave warriors such as the leader Zumbi. The stories of these characters are even still sung about in Capoeira songs.

The development of Salvador as a port also led to Capoeira being heavily practiced by the sailors who entered and left the city, and this too is still documented in songs. In the early 20th century, Salvador was the capital of Capoeira, and still was when it was legalised in the 1930s. Both the highly influential Grand Masters of Capoeira, Mestre Bimba and Mestre Pastinha trained in the city in these times, and thus Salvador's influence on Capoeira can't be overestimated. This also worked in reverse and Capoeira's influence on the city was also enormous. Rodas in the streets were commonplace and had fierce reputations. Many Mestres made their names in these rodas, and none were more famous than those at The Mercado Modelo.

This market had always hosted rodas and many had a reputation for being ruthless. It was a place where a Capoeirista could go and test his skills, but always with awareness of other street Capoeiristas. These Capoeristas would learn their Capoeira on the streets and stories were abounding of the use of knives and razors on unsuspecting opponents. These stories and Salvador's history had given me a large mixture of emotions. I was hugely excited at meeting the City's famous Masters and the old academies where so much had taken place. This was certainly mixed with a touch of nerves however, as Salvador's reputation was too large to ignore.

The Pelourinho is Salvador's main square and shows the city's past and future together. Here, many of the City's churches reside, along with the old slave trading buildings. However, the city's recent tourist boom now sees the square surrounded by souvenir shops, cafes and restaurants, and all under the eye of several police. The police, for fear of crime, keep many of the cities poorest children out, but not the many street sellers. As in the past, the square also still has rodas at most times of the day, many masters sell their berimbaus in the street. However, unlike the old days, all is now in the name of tourism.

Tom and I spent our first day in The Pelourinho. I was interested in buying some berimbaus and with a wary eye, I started to speak to Mestre Gaje. He knew both Gato and Peixinho and as always this turned out to be highly beneficial. As Tom began testing some poorly made berimbaus sold to unknowing tourists, Gaje, not wanting to offend a Gato student, began showing me his better berimbaus to try. Listening to Peixinho test his berimbaus in his workshop as well as being in many of his rodas, had given me a good idea of a nice berimbau sound (Peixinho's berimbaus always gave an excellent sound). I used this when deciding which were good and which were not so good. After some heavy bargaining, I had three for hundred Reais ($40), but possibly more importantly, Tom and I also had an invitation to Gaje's roda, the next day, in The Mercado Modelo. He assured us it would be safe.

Tom and I arrived early for the roda and took a look around the market whilst keeping a firm grip on our wallets. The concentration of tourists in one area meant there was more begging here than in Rio, especially outside the Pelourinho. We had discussed many things before deciding to go to the roda. A Danish friend had told us a story of someone recently being tesoured (a take down using the legs to twist the body to the floor) in the neck! Whether this was true or not, the Mercado Modelo had a reputation and we were a little nervous when we decided to go.

Gaje soon arrived and introduced us to the six students who he had brought with him. One he introduced as a Contra Mestre, and two were Formados (a graduated student). After the usual wait for some Brazilian organisation, the berimbau was finally ready and the roda began. The games were played on a stand, which was surrounded by two restaurants at the entrance to the market. I soon found out why. The opening games had all the intensity of swimming goldfish as the players exchanged kicks and esquivas in a bored, lazy style. They would then end with a show of a grab to the head and a handshake before two more players continued in a similar fashion. The Contra-Mestre's contribution was to enter the roda, look around, ginga and then walk out again.

The games weren't to get any better, and the music wasn't helping. The rodas 'energy' was being wholly created by one of the Formados and Tom. Gaje's contribution was perhaps most telling. He was on pandeiro. However, the only sound he made was shaking it to encourage tourists to enter their donations. Here showed the true reason behind the roda. Games were stopped at any moment for photos, and anyone caught filming or with a camera was soon met by Gaje's intimidating large figure 'requesting' a donation.

The sham all made a slight mockery of Tom and my fears, but it was clear that the students certainly knew how to deliver some vicious movements, and had a style which suggested they had learnt much from the street, with imperfect but effective technique. However, using one of these techniques would certainly cost them a few dollars in donations, and thus their wage. The roda's end couldn't arrive soon enough for Tom and myself, and it was no great surprise when another group turned up to start their own show. Two students even stayed and played again for another wage. Gaje thanked us for coming before giving me some advice on my game. "To win", he started, "use a Martello, a Bencao or chappa", all more direct kicks. He then gave Tom and myself our 50 cents wages before saying goodbye.

With so many of Salvador's residents practicing Capoeira, it is not surprising to know that there are numerous academies. The Pelourinho is full of Professors attempting to sell lessons to visiting gringos, but we already had a list of known academies and were determined to stick with what we had. The now arrived Jim and Miguel had decided to start lessons at Bimba's old academy, which was now being run by one of his sons, Mestre Bamba. Tom and I decided on the academy of another of Bimba's sons, Mestre Nenel.

Nenel let many of his lessons be run by students, in particular Pequeno Mestre, a small 18 year old. Bimba's influence in the academy was immediate, and one of the walls was covered with photos of many of his students. Of course, the teaching method was traditional, and strictly Regional.

After the now becoming common conversation over the groups pricing system, Nenel sat back and continued his game of patience on his computer. Pequeno Mestre soon had Tom and I stretching and then began showing us some movements. He decided to concentrate his lesson on Rastera (a sweep) and Tesoura (a scissor like take down with the legs). Tom and I were working hard, but Pequeno Mestre gave the class in good humour. We were also learning good technique, as we were the only students. We were certainly enjoying the close attention, but clearly not as much as forcing each other to the floor in the ways instructed. The concrete floor certainly gave our hands plenty to think about as we hit the ground each time.

The lesson ended with us playing and attempting rasteras when we could. Pequeno Mestre began to call a familiar tune for me though with his "Pull Raul, Pull!" as I continued to just show my Rastera. Gato was always warning me of this, and my only explanation was that I was too nice to pull! It didn't tend to be accepted.

Tom and I left the academy dripping with sweat and with a pledge to return for another lesson with Pequeno Mestre. Before our return, however, we had another famous academy to visit, and so we met with Miguel and Jim for a juice. They had been organising their schedule with Mestre Bamba and it seemed as though Jim's enthusiasm had perhaps got the better of him. He wanted to do six hours training a day, three in the morning and three in the afternoon. Having been trying what I thought was a packed schedule in Rio, I found this highly optimistic, but one had to admire his commitment. He and Miguel would start the next day.

Mestre João Peqeueno is a student of Mestre Pastinha, and though now in his 80s, still runs his Capoeira Angola academy just ten minutes walk from The Pelourinho. I had seen him in videos still doing cartwheels and kicks just a few years before and the respect he was given by other Masters was obvious.

A student of his called Alex greeted the four of us, and he was to take the lesson of about eighteen people. The lesson started with everyone playing the Angola rhythm on the berimbau, before starting the warm-up. This consisted of just two stretches. Firstly, pushing the hands to the ceiling, and then touching the toes. This was repeated several times before half an hour of hell was started for the knees. The class was told to ginga as low as possible, before moving to the floor in Negativa Angola (pushing the body to the floor on one side) and moving in a Rabo de arraia (a spinning kick with the body held low). The sequence was repeated with small variations until the arms could push the body to the floor no more, and my knees were crying to be stretched out. I was now beginning to understand why all Angoleirans had immensely toned shoulders.

The lesson continued with partners doing some movements together, but always with Alex close by. Only one pair did a sequence at any one time and in his friendly style, he corrected everything he didn't think was correct. I had never seen such close attention to detail and it was great to know that your technique was right.

Unfortunately, João Pequeno hadn't been at the lesson, but Alex said he would be at the roda on the coming Saturday.

After such a hugely impressive lesson, I was determined to go, and I knew the others were equally impressed.

Group Senzala practiced Angola but was more Regional in its training, so I saw Alex's lessons as a great opportunity to understand more of Capoeira Angola. Where better than the academy of Mestre João Pequeno, and I was even more convinced of this after speaking with Goodyear, a Dane I had met in Rio. He had been training at the academy for more than one month and said he had seen his Angola game improve with great leaps. I was eager to see more.

Though Jim had enjoyed the Angola class, his priority was his training at Bamba's academy and he was convinced that this was his first big chance to train his basics since he arrived, and he was determined to take it. A stomach bug was keeping me in bed so I waited for him to return after his first three hour session. After further 'evening success' for Miguel, he had decided to train for just one hour and thus returned earlier than Jim.

Miguel described the young student of Bamba's who was taking the class as "ruthless", and no one in the class stopped moving until the lessons ended. The lesson had been strict Regional, of course, and Miguel had kicked, dodged and sat up several hundreds of times. I was eager to see Jim and didn't have to wait long as he collapsed onto his bed. His three hours had been all Miguel had described, but multiplied by three, and he also added some of the slightly rough nature of the teaching after he had been bençoed to the floor by the teacher.

Despite this, Jim managed a further hour in the afternoon, and three hours the following day, until disaster struck on the third day. So far, Jim had been tesoured to the floor, thrown into some lockers and received a Martello into his face, and he hadn't even entered the roda yet! A kick to his ribs was too much, however. He had had trouble with them in England before and now his old injury returned. He was nothing short of livid with the teacher whom he had already told he was a beginner. He now joined me on the sidelines.

Tom had also taken some punishment at the academy. He shared my problem with flexibility and thus Bamba's young teacher had him stretching against the academy wall. Jim has admitted he had to admire him as his face turned purple and he screamed in agony. Though I laughed at missing out on this pain, my sadistic side was desperate to take a lesson at Bamba's and I made a promise not to leave Salvador until I had.

Miguel had a less suicidal approach to his training and had decided to mix his time between training at Bamba's, partying at Salvador's highly popular nightlife and making berimbaus in the Pelourinho. He had befriended a Mestre Cebolinha (little onion), who had agreed to teach him the art of making berimbaus. Miguel seemed quite content with his training, but I was becoming increasingly disillusioned. The constant offering of berimabaus, lessons, CD's or anything else a Capoeirista can sell was becoming tiresome. I even felt that some of the more traditional academies were somewhat cashing in on the influx of Gringo Capoeiristas, and who could blame them. However, I had arrived, perhaps naively, hoping to see some special rodas in the traditional capoeira surroundings, but I couldn't help feeling that much of the Capoeira had been turned into a business.

Shows, photos, t-shirts, lessons, berimabaus, pandeiros, videos, CDs. Everything was available at a price, and no chance was missed to let the gringos know it. Of course, we expected to pay for any training we did or things we bought, but I had also expected some friendship, interest in our Capoeira and as the Brazilians call it, Axe. Apart from Pequeno Mestre, the only academy I had found this was João Pequeno's and with this in mind, I was still excited about going to their weekly roda, and of course meeting the man himself.

Each group has there own way of oranising a roda. For example, Peixinho always had three berimabaus, one atabaque (drum) and one pandeiro (tambourine), where as Bamba's academy would use just one berimbau and two pandeiros, just as Bimba had done in the past. João Pequeno's roda consisted of three berimbaus, one atabaque, two pandeiros, one agogo and a reco-reco. The rhythms played were strictly those of Angola. João Pequeno was sitting at one end of the instruments and I introduced myself as a student of Gato and Senzala, and his nod and smile was my signal that I was accepted and could play. Like it seemed all great Masters had, he also had an aura, as if anyone would know that he was to be given special respect. Many people had told me that he was one of the great Capoeiristas and it was undoubtedly an honour to be shaking his hand and then play in his roda.

Angola games tend to be far longer than those in Regional, but like always, there are no set rules. The more playful and theatrical way of Angola leads it to be this way, with games often developing into fifteen or twenty minute encounters of brincando (joking). Of course, the fight is always present and no one knows when a smiling Capoeirista doing a slow Meu Lua de Frente will turn to do a fast Rastera. This led to the four gringo students waiting and singing a fair time before playing.

I watched Goodyear play with great interest and his game had developed hugely. He always had excellent technique, but now he was showing a great feel for the rhythm and his movements too.

Tom played a nice game with one of the academy's professors. I always thought Tom's Angola game was better than his regional and he looked more comfortable here than at Nenel's. Miguel's Angola game showed how much he had trained his Regional. I had always been told that playing Angola was never playing slow Regional, but Miguel played like this, and admitted as much. It was no surprise given the bias in his training over the years, but he was aware he needed to change.

Given my lack of training in Capoeira generally, I certainly didn't have this problem, but I did have a problem with understanding Angola. With my training in Rio, I was beginning to find more of an understanding of Regional. The rhythm, the flow of movements and the conversation as Mestre Toni liked to compare it. However, Angola was like another language to me. Someone had told me it was like becoming another person, just feeling the rhythm and playing. For the first time, I began to see what he meant. The game was more of a chess match with the players planning their moves with more time and patience. The players were also showing their personalities more than I had seen in Regional, joking and using more expressional movements. It is one thing to be told this in a class, but to see it for real, with music and energy your body can feel, not just hear, is different and I felt I was understanding more with each movement that passed.

When I played, I tried to keep to the rhythm of the game and ginga low, as I had been shown in the lesson. I also tried to break the continuity of the game as the Professors were doing so well. I felt a difference in my game and the watching Jim said he was impressed. Maybe Salvador was proving a disappointment to me, but the few lessons and this roda at João Pequenos taught me more than in any other week in Brazil. I was hugely grateful to Alex and the other teachers who had treated us so well and certainly hadn't seen us as dollar signs, but as other Capoeiristas wanting to learn.

With my stomach bug going and Salvador's wild Carnival arriving, I decided it was time to leave for Rio, but not before giving Mestre Bamba's class a try. The next morning I prepared for the worst.

Bimba's academy is a small hop from The Pelourinho and being on the first floor, overlooks one of Salvador's many cobbled streets. I arrived for a two hour lesson, but spent the first fifteen minutes just soaking in the academy itself. The many pictures and old newspaper cuttings on the walls reminded one of the traditions and Masters that had been created within. I read with interest of Bimba defeating many free fighters (he never lost a fight) in his younger days, and many photos showed some of the Masters he created.

It was a special feeling to train there, though after an hour, my body wasn't feeling particularly special. Jim's torturer was relentless in asking for more kicks and cartwheels as the class of six sweated all the water from their bodies. At one stage I was hopeful of a rest when my partner injured her foot, but an order of two hundred sit ups was soon forthcoming and destroyed my optimism. I was grateful for my intensive routine before in Rio and as the 2 hours ended with some very tired-looking games, my body was feeling like it felt at the end of a session by Gato's pool, very well worked and ready for a rest. I had missed the feeling throughout my time in Bahia and knew it was time to head back to my blood and guts training in Rio.

I noticed I was the only student to 'thank' the Professor as I left, but wasn't too surprised after he had left two students almost vomiting with exhaustion. After the traditional Brazilian meal of rice and beans, I had time to say goodbye to the others. Tom had decided to experience Carnival in the Northeast, where as Jim and Miguel wanted to continue their nightlife partnership after some recent success, before heading back to Rio. Tom helped me carry my bags and as my taxi left The Pelourinho, a small boy showed me a backflip before asking for some money, "just 10 cents amigo!!"

Chapter Twelve

Sou do Rio de Janeiro, sou do Rio de Janeiro Moco
(I'm from Rio, I'm from Rio my friend...Mestre Toni)

After another twenty seven hours on a bus, it was a nice feeling to cross the 13km Niteroi bridge and enter Rio de Janeiro once again. The city was beginning to feel like my home in Brazil, where I had my friends, and my teachers. One thing I hadn't missed however, was the dangers of the Favella, and with not having been there in over a month, I was a little nervous as to if there was a gang war currently happening. Mario, sitting in front of the house as always, was delighted with his T-shirt from Salvador and soon assured me that all was currently quiet and I was grateful that it seemed that even gangsters had a holiday at Carnival time.

Though the house wasn't experiencing an invasion of gangsters, another invasion had taken place. Camarao had also returned to the house, but he wasn't alone. Eight other Danes had also joined him in what Jim later termed 'the Viking invasion'. Most were only to stay for Carnival before heading off to different parts of the country, though Camarao was certainly the leader. Though Ia had also returned, Camarao now had some knowledge of Portuguese and knew some of the geography of the city. His skills in percussion had impressed even the Brazilians at the event in Ilheus, and being with a grey cord, which was unusual for foreigners, was certainly being held in high esteem by his counterparts.

He had decided to buy tickets for the main Sambadrome, where the world's most famous Carnival would take place. With so many tourists entering Rio for this week, ticket prices were becoming higher with every day, and I was soon realising that Carnival in this city was more for the tourists, and the locals travelled outside. I had been told that Carnival in Rio was different from the rest of Brazil in that it was more of a show. The beat varied from city to city, but in Rio it was strictly samba, the costumes as loud and wild as possible and the crowd gringos or richer Brazilians.

I had decided to meet with the returning Jim and Miguel and party in Terrarao, one of the parties which surrounds the Sambadrome. The streets were full of people in the most wild costumes I had ever seen, with a fantastic range of colours. Bright blues, greens and yellows fought for my attention along with the sounds of samba on huge stereos, and somewhat unbelievably, beer sellers who still made themselves heard. The trucks that would pass through the Sambadrome were decorated just as wildly as the people they were transporting, and my particular favourite was a giant eagle of what seemed a fifteen metre wingspan. I was beginning to realise how the Brazilians spent a whole year preparing for the event.

Carnival lasts for five days and in Rio, it is actually a competition. Only Brazil could turn Samba into a competitive event and each Samba school prepares meticulously in its attempt to win. I guess it adds an extra spice, as if any was needed, to the party. For me, each was equally impressive. I also had to be impressed by the fireworks that would light up the Rio sky every hour or so for five nights. It certainly was the biggest party in the world.

With Carnival being a holiday all over Brazil, lessons were off for the week. It was a shame as I was eager to get back into my old routine I had worked on before my trip to Bahia. As always, Jim was equally keen. He had recovered from his rib problem and was now in Brazil for only one purpose, training. He decided he should move into the Favella once the Danes had gone, which would not only place him nearer to Gato's house, and hence morning training, but also further from Miguel, who was planning to head home soon anyway after feeling he had run out of women in Brazil!

As Carnival finished, and the Danes moved on, just Camarao and his friends, Mads and Daniel stayed on. Jim moved in and morning training was back on the menu. Jim and I began rising before 7am to start before Rio's summer heat became too much. Gato was keen to take a closer look at Jim and came to some of our earlier sessions, leaving us as always with a pad at hand. I began in earnest showing Jim all the combinations that I had been doing on the pad and how my kicks had improved in control and speed. He was eager to learn.

Once Gato had left us each morning, Jim and I would turn the stereo up some notches and get kicking. At first we tried to do fifty of each kick. Jim was keen to improve his armada and so always started with this before beginning to get angry at about number forty with the odd stumble on one side. Something all Capoeiristas have are good and bad sides with the majority of movements. I always preferred doing cartwheels on my left side, and my right leg was generally stronger on most kicks. This frustration and the inevitable "but I can do it really well on that side!" is undoubtedly annoying, but perhaps more annoying is the need to train more movements on the bad side. This when really all one wants to do is train a movement the best they can do (i.e. the best side). This is where having a training partner inevitably helps and Jim and I were always willing partners.

After several sets of kicks on the pad, we then pushed out the requisite dips, push ups and sit ups before a quick swim and then home for an extremely large and deserved breakfast. Jim and I had agreed to try and keep to this routine for as long as we could with only resting at weekends.

However, we always knew this would be hard to do with the evening lessons too, but I was just happy I had found someone as suicidal in his training as myself, but Jim was soon to learn that this isn't always the best way.

With a large batizado about to occur in Denmark, it meant many of the Senzala Mestres were preparing to leave for Europe again. Most organised to visit many countries in one trip and with this in mind, Toni had already left. I was a little disappointed by this as Jim and I had started to attend many more of his classes. His more open teaching style than Peixinho appealed to Jim, and I always found his class a little more inviting. We tried to see Peixinho once a week and Toni twice, with Gato's lessons in between.

Gato was another preparing to leave for Europe, as well as Peixinho, and so we were left to wonder who would take the classes. Peixinho left Azeite in charge, but over the coming weeks various Professors took his class. Gato's less formal class was to be taken by his daughter Paula, and Toni decided to leave his to Lobo. Though it was disappointing to see the Mestres leave, Jim and I were curious as to how these future Mestres would be.

In fact, Jim had more pressing things to worry about. Our heavy morning training schedule, an average workout was beginning to hit four hours, was taking its toll on his feet. All sports tend to have regular annoyances or injuries associated with them, and Capoeira was no different. The constant twisting on the foot, often without shoes, left the skin on the feet in a filthy state and blistering was common. I had suffered badly on my trip with Medusa when Suassuna had jokingly told me off for wearing trainers. In order to prove a point, I switched to bare feet and paid the consequences with weeks of agony until my skin hardened.

Jim was now in a similar situation, and even wearing trainers wasn't helping. Each Armada made Jim grimace in more pain and thus it was clear, he either found a short term solution or stop and let his feet heal. Mads was to prove helpful. He had bought some special blister plasters from Denmark, which grooved onto the foot perfectly to stop them falling off. The protection lasted for two days, but left the blister in the same state as no air was getting to the foot. Jim decided to favour a more natural solution.

We were training with our pad as always when Jim pulled up again holding his foot and claiming he would have to stop again. He then hopped off to the bathroom, as I made the most of the break. Just ten minutes had passed before Jim was ready again. "How's the foot then?" I asked, expecting a big grumble, however, it seemed to be remarkably healed. I wanted the secret and Jim's preference to getting to the point quickly meant I didn't have to wait for too long. "Well, I pissed on it" he said.

Now taking a pee on one's foot I heard was a good idea when stung by a jellyfish but for blisters? But I couldn't claim it hadn't worked. The blister had gone hard, if a little yellow, and Jim was feeling no pain at all. " That's something that should be passed on to any student by his Master" I claimed as once again the pad was taking our best shots.

With this new method of surviving his blisters, Jim and I were keen to see what the young Senzala professors had in store in the evening lessons. When Peixinho had last gone to Europe, I noticed that many of his students stopped coming to class, and once again this was to be the case. Azeite gave a very similar lesson in style with sequences given to a leading student to show the rest of the class before everyone doing it together to the sound of the berimbau. However, his sequences tended to be longer than those Peixinho gave, and thus many people seemed to be struggling to pick them up. In fact, it was often taking just ten minutes to get everyone to know the sequence before actually doing it. The class would go on to some sequences in pairs and then a roda, which although having less energy than the usual Peixinho rodas, were always well received.

The second week of Peixinho's absence did see a very different lesson given. Professor Chiquinho arrived from the other side of Rio and gave a fantastic lesson. He started with some warm-up exercises before moving down the hall using the queda da rins movements that his game relied on. I had often watched the way he moved so graciously around the roda, and I felt that much of this was his use of Queda da rins (break to the ribs). This movement helps the body arrive at the floor with control by slowly moving the elbow into the ribs. Chiquinho showed the movement in various situations using cartwheels and kicks. I noticed Jim, who had a very good Queda da rins, picking Chiquinho's brains on the exact technique of each movement and he was only too happy to help.

The lesson ended with everyone being forced to sing one line of a song before a roda. The nature of the lesson had been highly relaxed and I always found this led to the best rodas afterwards. In this way, no one feels inhibited and all feel very much a part of what is happening. Some other Peixinho students were always on hand to help with the music as some of the lower cords took the chance to play. This included Eric.

Though many of Senzala's characters trained with Gato, Eric was a regular at Peixinho's class, along with his son, Ericinho (little Eric). Eric was a mix of Brazilian and Swedish, and spoke excellent English due to previously living in the US as a doctor. He had befriended the Danes since they had arrived and was helping them where he could.

In Capoeira, Eric only had a white cord, but always showed determination not to be dominated by anyone in the roda, and that meant even the highest of cords. Eric would swing his slightly uncoordinated body almost ignoring any of the kicks that were coming his way, determined to close the gap on the other player and use his hands. His exceedingly baggy white trousers would flap as he did his kicks in the roda, and then attempt to run at his opponent and fell him. His style was unique, but did prove that any one of any age could find something in Capoeira.

This particular Chiquinho roda proved two things. Firstly, Eric was still ignoring kicks in the roda, and secondly, Jim's potential as a Capoeirista. Eric often chose to play the gringos in a gesture of friendship and this time he bought Jim's game. However, his style could be infuriating as it led to a highly influid game, and Jim was clearly becoming frustrated. As he went to the floor, Eric ran in again to close his space. Jim instinctively kicked hard and fast from the floor, and his foot whisked through Eric's blondie-grey hair. The kick surprised all in the roda and showed Jim's enormous flexibility, as well as his intuition for the game. I was delighted for him, and pleased for Eric too, that he could still use his highly developed brain.

After the class, Eric announced that he had managed to help Camarao and Daniel find an apartment in Copacabana. The dangers of the Favella had persuaded the two Danes to move, and with Mads finalising his flight back to Denmark, the house was about to become more spacious. Though Camarao was especially excited about moving toward the beach of Copacabana, I had no feelings of jealousy. I always found Copacabana the worst area to be in. With the long beach and mountains encasing the area the only way to build was up, which meant Copacabana was full of high rise apartment blocks and hotels (it has the highest population density of any district in the world). It was the district of the tourist, which meant all the things that came with that. Bars, clubs, conmen, traffic and hookers.

The beach was long and full of activity but I always preferred Ipanema. There was less hassling of any gringos, more modern buildings and an all round more relaxing atmosphere. If it hadn't been so far for morning training, this would have been my choice for a place to live.

As it was, the Favella was still Jim and my residence and we had been making slightly more friends in the area. One neighbour had made the effort to come and converse with me, and with my ever-improving language skills, I made a good job of being friendly. His warning of not making any trouble, however, was highly unnecessary as I had no intention of causing anyone harm, especially the chaps with Uzis.

There was also the old man on the steps who seemed to always be sitting outside his house and always obliged with a hello, and then the lady who sold sweets at the top of the steps who always had a smile for the Favella's gringos. Whether it was because we were Peixinho's friends or because we were gringos, it didn't really matter to Jim and myself, as the main point was that people were being friendly.

This atmosphere gave us slightly more confidence and though we bought the majority of our food at a supermarket near Gato's house, for odd items we started to venture into the local Favella shop. Though it was only fifty metres from the house, the shop was situated further into the Favella and thus within a closer distance of the drug dealers at the bottom of the street. With the weather becoming increasingly hot, Jim and I would take it in turns on ice lolly trips. The female owner was always on hand with a welcoming smile and it spoke further of Favella life as she always had friends around chatting whilst she worked.

After training one morning at Gato's house, it was my turn for the ice lolly run, and a run is how it almost very much turned out. As I walked down the street I caught a glimpse of a teenager hiding behind the corner of a house. As I approached further however, my heart began to race as he held his revolver up in the street whilst listening to his walkman. Though I knew he wasn't waiting for me, the feeling of crossing a revolver's shot path is not one that I wanted to take too often. I decided to carry on, but soon realised I would have to return and pass again. The lollies were good, but I could survive with cold water.

I picked up and paid for the lollies without really thinking about their flavour. I tried to walk back calmly and didn't want to make eye contact with the teenager, who was still at his posting. A golden rule was never to run in the

Favella, as making someone with a gun nervous is never wise, and especially when they are young, and most likely a lot more scared than you are. I walked and concentrated on the end of the road like never before, as if other gangsters were coming, I certainly wasn't planning to hang around in the crossfire.

The gunman's youth was of no great surprise to me. With families in the Favellas earning so little money the temptation to earn 50 reais a day (about $17) to hold a gun at a gunpost is often more tempting than school for many. Most drugdealers don't live past 24. The gunman probably assumed I was a rich gringo picking up some drugs, and would undoubtedly had been shocked to find two ice lollies in my bag if he looked. He had no interest though and I made it back safely to greet Mario, before running up and telling Jim my story. He instinctively grabbed me a new pair of underpants!

Despite my latest Favella story, Tom's arrival from the North East saw him also move into the house. He had experienced Carnival in Salvador and Recife and had returned for some intensive training before heading back to Scotland. His first lesson was to be that of the Favella rules before we headed to Mestre Toni's class, which was currently being taken by Professor Lobo, in the district of Flamengo.

Lobo had become one of my favourite players in Senzala, despite his previous experiment with Harry Krishna music. His training with Toni meant that he had less of Peixinho's style than many of Senzala's higher cords, but was equally as fast and skilled. His long dark hair bounced as he did his ginga with great fluidity, and he also gave more expression in his movements than many others.

As always, his class began with a warm-up that tried to break the mould of normal warm-ups. Whether it was using different rhythms, or running round a local children's playground, the unexpected was always round the corner. Lobo was also keen to attempt to introduce many sequences not usually done in Toni's class, and with this in mind, we started to train the bridge sequences that Mestre Suassuna had made so famous, and I had seen so many times in Sao Paulo and Fortaleza.

Unfortunately, this didn't mean that I was especially good at them. Jim had taught me some exercises to increase my back flexibility, but like all stretching, the effects take time to see and so I had to be patient and attempt the movements the best I could. On a concrete floor however, this was proving painful. As I went into a bridge, my back would give way and I would crash to the floor. I would do this several more times until Lobo showed some more movements I could struggle with.

With Tom's lack of flexibility causing him similar problems, Jim was to steal the show. He could enter a bridge with ease and would then spin out better than many of the Brazilians. Whilst I became frustrated, Jim became more and more excited with what he was learning.

These lessons were to continue in this way for the whole duration of Toni's absence, but I couldn't deny that the new movements weren't enjoyable to train. As fun as Toni's group were to train with, any roda would miss Toni's energy, and so it was to be here. His songs were still sung with gusto and enthusiasm and the rodas were certainly still enjoyable, but Toni's voice was always missing.

This didn't mean, of course, that the rodas standard of play was worse. Lobo, Doburu and Toni's other professors always played to a high standard. A newer student had also become a regular, and his name was Caculee. He had arrived from Minas Gerais to train specifically with Toni, but in his Mestre's absence he had decided to have some fun with the gringo students, especially with Tom.

Caculee was quick, and had obviously been training many of Peixinho's sequences of feinting movements before entering with a throw or a sweep. These were too good for us, and time and time again he was leaving us on the floor. It was Tom who was to take the worst of it though. It seemed each roda Caculee would play him and throw him down, and when Tom got up to play again, another kick would come his way. I could never really understand players who felt the need to prove themselves against weaker players. Maybe it was insecurity, or just plain old fashioned bullying, but like all bullies, there is always someone bigger.

The next roda was to prove just that as Caculee started playing another Brazilian and took him down with a sweep. I could see Tom's relief, as he knew it wasn't just him. This expression however, was soon overtaken with happiness as Caculee was soon put to the floor with a hard kick from his opponent. Jim's shout of "well he had that coming" was fortunately not understood by any of the Brazilians in the roda, but it summed up how we felt.

The good news was that more was to come when Toni arrived back from his trip. All his students were very excited and the roda had enormous energy. The games were picking up in pace when Caculee again bought Tom's game. I could sense some nervousness in Tom, and rightly so as after just a minute, Caculee had kicked him five metres outside the roda. Toni interrupted immediately and brought his student to the berimbau for a slapped wrist as Tom brushed himself down. The game restarted with Caculee playing a far less aggressive and simpler game.

This wasn't the end for Tom however, who I saw kicked and thrown many more times in various rodas in Rio. Gato said it was Tom's closed playing style, which many people took as awkward and slightly imposing. I never could come to an answer, but knew that if anything, it showed that Capoeira certainly wasn't just a pretty dance.

Chapter Thirteen

Vamos jogar Capoeira, Vamos tocar berimbau
(Lets go play Capoeira, lets go play berimbau...Popular)

With the intensity of my training in Brazil, I was always aware of attempting to rest my body, eat well and drink plenty of water. I was very good at the second two, but often found the first frustrating. My mind was set that I was in Brazil to train, and learn as much as I possibly could, and this contributed to any breaks from training as feeling like wasted time. I also found it intensely frustrating to watch a roda in which I couldn't participate, and also with training. When I had in the past been sick or carrying an injury, I had often told Gato of how I felt a little of how alchoholism might be. Sitting in a pub watching everyone drink knowing you could, but only with great pain afterwards. As for playing the berimbau, which I was enjoying more and more, that to me was like drinking orange juice. You are involved but not how you want to be. It was a poor analogy in truth, but the best I could do.

Overall, I had been relatively lucky with injuries throughout my training. I had had many problems in England, but only the odd muscle pull or cold in Brazil. However, I had a long-term injury in my hip, that no sepcialist had ever managed to resolve (much to my martellos frustration) and at times it gave me great pain. However, now it was starting to deteriorate, and I was beginning to miss the odd session. I decided to continue with the policy I had kept to througout my time, wait and see.

The problem was being kept to the back of my mind by two things; the imminent arrival of the Senzala Mestres from their travels and the return of button football with Gabriel.

Though my debts were starting to mount, I still thought I could spare enough for a new button football table, and so 20 Reais later, Gabriel and my rivalry was to return. We soon found our favourite players once again and were returning to our previous high standards within days, though suspiciously Gabriel seemed to have improved even though we hadn't played the game for several months. He was to take the opening exchanges.

Perhaps more interesting was Gato's return with Peixinho following a few days later. Gato had had an eventful trip including visits to France, England, Scotland and Denmark. Pedro had organised a batizado in Edinburgh, and a Peixinho student, Steen, had organised a similar event in Copenhagen. Gato spoke highly of each, but especially the event in Copenhagen, where Steen had almost 200 students. He had invited teachers from all over Europe and Brazil and it had ended with a grand party that Beatrice had clearly also enjoyed.

At the forefront of the party was Camarao, who had returned home to collect his blue cord. He had trained well in his time in Brazil and deserved his new level, but I had fears that some of his success was beginning to go to his head. It was understandable. Camarao was still just 18 years of age, and had the confidence and the talent to attempt to match the Brazilians at everything they did.

In the roda, he sang and led the energy whilst playing the berimbau excellently, and his Capoeira had improved to make him a faster and all round better player. In Ilheus he had impressed all with his skills on the drums, and now his Portuguese was improving too. For someone of such a young age there was always the danger it would go to his head. He began playing with a hint of arrogance, walked with an air of authority and much to Gabriel's annoyance, began missing Gato's class. Gabriel saw this as a large lack of respect for his father and started telling me how he would take Camarao down in a roda when he saw him.

I tended to agree. Having seen Camarao arrive in Brazil as a quiet and polite youngster with enthusiasm to learn all he could, I was now seeing him more as someone who had learnt much, but was keen to show it to everyone who could see. I thought it was fanatastic that he had developed so well, but was hoping that with time he would become more humble. I was certainly having less contact with him since he had moved out the favella, but was still seeing him in Peixinho's class (which he now positioned himself at the front of), and hoped Peixinho would guide him as best he could.

After Gato had given Jim, Tom and myself an account of their journey, he invited us to morning training the next day. I could see he had been slightly inspired by his travels, especially, it seemed, by his time in Copenhagen. The next morning was to show this even further. We arrived at the usual time of 7am to be met with an especially enthusiastic Gato. He had already been stretching, and within minutes we had joined him. After running through Bimbas sequences, (Gato liked to finish the warm-up with these) we then trained some sequences Gato had picked up in Copenhagen. I always liked this about Gato. Though he had trained for many years, he was always willing to try new movements or ways of training.

He worked us hard and we decided to all have breakfast together afterwards. Within minutes the talk was back to Capoeira and Gato was suggesting I tried some more movements in the roda. He meant more throws and sweeps. For months he had warned me to throw in more definitive movements like this, and most importantly, to follow them through and not just show them as was my habit. My training had shown me when to use them, all I needed now was to practice physically doing them in the roda.

I was determined to spend my final weeks in Brazil playing as much as possible and with Gato's advice, I was going to attempt what I always thought impossible, to catch out some professors. I decided to start that night in Peixinho's roda.

With Peixinho only recently returning, all the students who had been training elsewhere whilst he had been abroad returned to his lessons, and the roda was once again a ball of energy and sound. The windows of the academy were always closed at this point so the sounds didn't interrupt the neighbours.

Cutia started the games and showed how much he was improving. I had seen him in my opening week in Rio and had decided to measure my progress against his, but I had underestimated his talent by a long way. He had developed at an enormous rate over my time there, with his flexible body allowing him to move in ways that others in the academy struggled with. This didn't mean that he had less of the Senzala style, however. He was always looking to enter in close to his opponent, and had a dangerous sweep and throw. His problem however, came through being so light. His tiny body meant his was easily pushed around in the roda by bigger players, but he was developing great speed to counteract this.

The roda saw many Professors including Guarda Costas (bodyguard). He was another student of Peixinho who I had watched with interest through my time there. He was one of the most powerful men I had ever seen with muscles and bulk bulging from all over his body. I often saw him practicing his punching movements, which shook the kick bags at the end of a lesson. His bulk also made him slow however, and with this in mind I chose him to practice my movements on.

I bought his game with Gato's advice from the morning ringing in my ears. My morning training often included kicking and then entering for a throw and now I looked for an opportunity. I waited for the right moment and threw a spinning armada kick. The bulk in front of me responded as I had hoped, with his own kick, and I entered into the perfect position to throw him in a movement named Vigitiva. In that split second, I felt a mix of emotions. Firstly, I was enormously happy at having managed to enter in on a professor, but secondly, more surprised. I was to be even more surprised however, when I saw a large fist heading for my nose.

My habit for just showing a movement and not actioning it had meant I had stopped short of unsettling the large body next to me. My punishment was a shown fist on my nose, which gave me more shock than pain. I had amused the watching Tom however, who found my slight frame trying to throw a giant a hilarious contradiction. I was happy though. My training had allowed me to surprise a good Capoeirsta, even if I didn't take him to the ground like I did in my mind. I knew I would have plenty more opportunities before my time was up.

With Gato's enthusiasm still bubbling, morning training was to have an extra twist over the coming weeks. He had decided the time was right to teach Jim, Tom and myself the Cintura Desprezada. This was a further training of the late Mestre Bimba and involved a series of throws by each student. The students needed to work together for one to jump, and the other to throw with great timing. For safety, and a nice view, Copacabana beach was chosen.

The four of us started to arrive there at 7am for an early start. We would warm-up in the usual manner and then Gato took us through each throw. One involved holding a handstand whilst the other grabbed the hips and threw his opponent over his shoulder. Another involved grabbing the neck and rotating the opponent's body 180 degrees over the others shoulder. Gato demonstrated with me, though I was doing little of the work. We would then try the movements together.

The first attempts ended up with both players in the sand on their backsides and Gato was clearly enjoying himself. Jim was picking it up slightly faster than Tom or myself, but it needed both players to work together to complete the movements well. This was proving difficult. After Tom almost piledrived me into the sand wrestling style, Gato decided to call it a day. We would return tomorrow.

With my student visa close to ending and my financial situation becoming worse with each week, I was thinking more and more about where to go next. Rio had enchanted me in every way. The constant sunshine, beautiful views at every corner and relaxed nature of life was so contrary to my previous life in England, but had proved to be very much to my liking. The novelty of being in Brazil had disappeared some months ago, and it was feeling more homelike with each week that passed. I was even more enthusiastic about my Capoeira than when I had arrived and was finally starting to show true improvements in my Portuguese. If there was a way of staying I wanted to know of it and so my search began.

Teaching English is always an option anywhere in the world and with this I visited more than fifteen schools in Rio for potential jobs. However, visas were always an issue, as was the pay. The strength of foreign currency was improving all the time as the Brazilian Real began dropping in value, and thus any work outside of Brazil would prove highly more beneficial than working within the country. Again, I decided to sit on my thoughts and concentrate on other matters. Most importantly the state of my ever worsening hip, and the imminent departure of Jim.

Jim had spent three months experiencing so much of what Brazil had had to offer. His Capoeira had improved enormously and he had enjoyed his time in and out of Rio. I was especially sad to see him go. He had proved my closest ally and best training partner throughout my time, but though I knew I would miss his influence, I knew I had a camarada for a long time to come. He left and we promised to meet at an upcoming event in Newcastle in the North East of England.

Fortunately, Tom was to remain for a further month, and thus Gato still had his students to practice the Cintura, and he asked us to give a demonstration of the sequence at the upcoming event. As we were still driving each other's heads into the sand, it was a big thing to ask, but Tom was keen so we agreed. Copacabana beach was about to become our morning home.

Though progress was slow, Tom and I were improving and understanding more of the sequence. Sometimes we would find our timing perfect and the body being thrown would literally fly through the air almost effortlessly. It was a great feeling, but not one we were to become too acustomed to, as my hip was deteriorating rapidly. The training I had done over the months was taking its toll, and now my pain was starting to effect my basic movements. I was beginning to pull up in morning training doing a series of kicks or sweeps, or even sometimes when I trained my ginga. It was clear I had to stop and seek some help.

Tom was dissapointed about not being able to practice the Cintura but understood my reasons. Gato sent me to his physio, who began working on my posture, and I also went to see Eric. He said he had a friend who was an orthapedic surgeon and he would help me.

I was keen to see his friend as soon as possible and he so he took me to the hospital where he worked. I had never entered a Brazilian hospital before, and though I had become accustomed to people staring at me from my time in the North East, I was certainly the centre of attention in the waiting room. Gringos in public Brazilian hospitals were obviously not very common.

I explained in a mixture of English and Portuguese my pains to the specialist, who then took some x-rays, but found nothing. According to him, my months of pain was nothing more than a muscle problem that I should stretch and rest for two weeks. I was dubious. I had spent months stretching the pain and had seen numerous specialists who hadn't managed to solve the problem. It didn't seem possible that it was something as simplistic as a muscle problem, but I was becoming desperate and took his advice on board.

I had already stopped training for the previous two weeks and it had been the usual frustrating time.I had watched lessons, and practiced berimbau until my fingers hurt, but as always, I wanted to throw some kicks, beat a pad and ginga in a roda again. I found it easy to feel a little dramatic at times, after all, this was training and not a matter of life or death, but also began to understand how professional athletes can feel through periods of injury. When training becomes such an intense part of someone's life, it is more important than just a sport. It becomes part of the make-up of that person, part of their personality and character. Taking this away would effect the strongest of people. I was however, determined this wouldn't be the end of my training in Brazil and decided to find other ways of learning.

I began spending more time in the house, and was fortunate as Peixinho and Ramos were busy making berimbaus. With my improving Portuguese I was able to ask them more questions of Capoeira, and Peixinho, who had suffered a serious knee injury in the past, was especially sympathetic.

I watched any rodas I could, and Peixinho's latest Roda of the month was as good as always. Chiquinho and one of his students showed how the Cintura sequence could be done as they flew through the air, and the games were of an especially high quality.

My other method was to tap into Gato's video collection. With Beatrice's love of photography and film, they had collected tens of videos of rodas and events from the years. Though Gato began to worry over my obsessive behaviour, I decided to catalogue them one by one. I found things I never imagined existed.

I found footage of some of the greatest masters, singing, talking and playing. Some days were better than others, but occasionally I struck gold and found some forgotten footage of Mestre Joao Pequeno or other such greats.

On my sixth day I found exactly what I was looking for. Mestre Boneco was one of the originators of Capoeira Brasil, which was now one of the leading groups in the world. Though he now taught in Los Angeles, he had taught in Rio in the past and this video I had chosen at random was of one of his Batizados from the early 1990s. Beatrice had filmed the master's roda, which included such illustrious names such as Mestres Joao Pequeno, Gato, Peixinho, Suassuna, Itapoan, Mao Branca and many more. It was like watching a whos who of the Capoeira world, and Beatrice was always on hand to put names to faces.

This roda in particular gave me enormous inspiration. Firstly there was Mestre Eziquel, who did the singing in the roda. He had been a former student of Mestre Bimba's and sung with a voice like no other I had heard. It gave the roda something different. Something that anyone, Capoeirsta or not, could appreciate.

The roda also showed my old friend from the North East, Mestre Espirro Mirim. Within seconds of his entering the roda I was entranced. He moved with a fluidity I had never seen from anyone, and his style was nothing short of beautiful. When an attack came, he closed like a hedgehog rolling away and then swiftly entering once again with grace and speed. As the roda's rhythm became faster, this opening and closing became even more exaggerated, and he even added the two most graceful jumps I had ever seen. I rewound the tape again and again, but knew I had found something not just impressive, but truly inspirational.

I found more footage over the remaining weeks that also left an impression on me, but nothing like this roda, or Mestre Espirro's movement. It had been implanted on my mind, and if I could teach myself to move anything like he could, I would become a happy Capoeirista. I had heard it said that everyone's path in Capoeira is different as people take influence from different places. I was beginning to understand more and more where I wanted to go next in my training, and watching the various masters on the tapes was helping considerably.

Chapter Fourteen

Eu vou me embora, Boa Viagem…
(I'm going away, Have a good trip….Popular)

Throughout my time in Brazil, Gabriel had been a major annoyance. He was the adolescent with too much time on his hands, who would laugh at my attempts with Capoeira and Portuguese, and argue his every point to exhaustion. He had however, become a close friend. Beatrice had compared us to brothers who would argue all day, but still accompany one another for hours.

He had matured over the months, but wasn't losing his sense of humour, which was still as poignant as ever. His Capoeira had reached a good level, which with more training could become very good, but it was in his guitar playing that Gabriel saw his future. He would practice for several hours a day, and his level was improving with each week. One had to admire his commitment.

With both of us being highly competitive, we knew that my final week was fast arriving, and also knew the significance. Our year of button football matches was heading to a final championship, and Gabriel was in confident mood and he had every reason to be. Since we had bought the new table, he had won eight of the last ten games. Even my top scorer was struggling and I was worried. Leaving Brazil with Gabriel as champion would be soul destroying. We decided not to play again until the end, which would be the ultimate game.

Tom never quite had the same interest in football, but was throwing all his efforts into his training. Like me, he was still struggling with his flexibility, but at least he didn't have Caculee to worry about anymore. I would often go to training with him to watch the rodas. Contra Mestre Xango from Capoeira Brasil had contacted Gato, and he had started training and bringing students to Gato's class. Xango was a very good Capoeirista and would get to prove himself in the next roda.

The great Angola master, Mestre Jogo de Dentro, was in Rio and came to visit Gato. Peixinho came with some students and thus the roda was set. Jogo de Dentro played some Angola games with Peixinho and the respect was obvious. He then came and joined me on the berimbau as the rhythm became faster.

I had been practicing my berimbau over my whole time in Brazil, but especially in the previous month of my injury. My playing was becoming better, and more in time. Playing in the roda however, was the true test. The berimbaus should play together in the roda, keeping the rhythm, whilst allowing the individual players to add to the sound as they see fit. Each player therefore had to listen to the others to make the music as strong as they could, and help the energy of the roda.

I was now playing with a Master, not just of Capoeira, but also of music. It wasn't unusual for me, as I had heard Ramos and Peixinho playing several times, but now I was playing *with* the Master. I kept to the rhythm as best I could whilst listening to how Jogo de Dentro played his berimbau. I felt a focus on the music that I never had before, understanding how the individuals went away from each other before heading back to the rhythm once again. For once, the pain a berimbau can give to one's finger was secondary to the feeling of being a true part of the roda, and making sure the energy was as good as it could be. I began to see that this was an art in itself.

The games that were happening in front of me were eye catching enough for my attention not to be completely lost. Tom played Xango in a nice game. He was lucky to play a Contra Mestre who would play at his opponent's level, whilst never losing his style and composure. Peixinho then bought the game.

I was interested to see the game. Xango had proved to be a very good Capoeirista, but Peixinho was still a test for anyone. They exchanged movements with Xango visibly raising his game several gears. He then managed to achieve something very rare. He caught Peixinho. Peixinho spun a fast kick at Xango, who moved backwards before launching both feet at the master whilst on one hand. Peixinho was clearly surprised, but like Gato had told me many times, everyone gets caught sometimes.

The game continued and Peixinho was clearly not finished yet. Camarao had told me that every Capoeirista should have two or three options for each situation that can occur, but that Peixinho had ten! With this in mind a fast spinning kick caught Xango unaware and he just managed to avoid it. Peixinho then came out with one of his favourites, a fake Martello that sent his opponent one way, and then his foot would change direction and catch his opponent's face. I had never seen anyone avoid it, until now.

Like all, Xango went to his right to avoid the upcoming foot, however, when it quickly changed direction he managed to move his body out of the way and down to a Rastera on Peixinho's foot. He didn't have time to pull him down, but Peixinho was clearly impressed. So was I. They ended the game with a show of respect in an embrace. It was Capoeira at its very best.

As Gato gave a lift to Tom and myself after the class, we had other things on our mind. Tom had always been less worried over the dangers of Brazil than myself. Maybe it was his lack of a bad experience, but sometimes I found him taking for granted where we were. There was always much exaggeration through books and television over Rio's dangers, and avoiding much of it was a simple case of commonsense, but no one could deny it existed. Tom would enter streets or alleys without hesitation, never seeming to stop to think where he was.

After a year of warnings and experiences, I would take nothing for granted, and that was especially true of the Favella. In Jim's final week, gang warfare had started like none I had experienced. The Red Command was currently in control of the Favella, but the Third Command (the other large gang of Rio) seemed determined to take it. Each night rivals were entering the Favella and shooting at each other in front of Peixinho's house. This made the walk into the Favella even more nerve-racking than normal, and I was often waiting at the top of the stairs for some minutes before entering.

Over time I had become so accustomed to hearing shots at night that I didn't even wake-up and would be told the next day, however, some nights in the previous week were far worse than normal. The night before had seen a large attack. I was awoken at 2am by shouts coming from the street. Though I couldn't understand what was being said, it was clear an attack was imminent. The shots a few minutes later were confirmation. There were obviously several involved, and I guess they had entered from the staircase. In the distance, and not for the first time, I heard a grenade explode.

Though I had become more accustomed with time to the firing of guns so near, my heart always began to race when it started. This night was worse though and the shootout continued for over twenty minutes before the inevitable happened. The police arrived and a barrage of more shots was fired. I resisted the temptation to peek over the balcony, but my open window meant I could hear everything clearly, as the police attempted to clear the road of bandits.

Another thirty minutes passed before I could return to sleep, but this clearly wasn't a war that was going to end soon. I was always aware however, that I was returning to safe England soon, and could go back at any point I wanted. How different it was for the thousands in Rio who had no choice but to live with such violence on their streets. I always remembered the group of school children who had befriended me who lived further into the Favella. When I was gone they would still be awoken each night by the sounds of gang warfare, and would still have to pass the gunmen on their way to school. It wasn't just Capoeira that Brazil was teaching me.

The continuing wars always took up space in the morning newspapers and this battle was actually big enough to earn some inches the next day. However, it had been demoted into second place, as once again the main motorways to the airport had been closed the previous evening due to further shootouts between police and a nearby Favella. This was soon to be followed by a six-hour shootout the next day where one police vehicle (some might call them tanks) was exploded by the bandits. I couldn't help being grateful that hadn't happened in front of Peixinho's house too.

Commentators were always on hand to offer analysis, but I never read a solution. The Rio head of police had been changed again, but I could see little of what he could do. Poverty had caused people to turn to crime, drugs had caused people to seek guns, and low pay had caused many police to turn to corruption. It was a formula for a long running war that would continue long after I left Rio, and possibly forever. It was also a war that not many from outside Brazil would ever see, or perhaps hear of, but I didn't think it would do much harm to have many Europeans spend a week in a Favella in Brazil. The sounds, people, energy and friendship have been fostered by hardship, but I always thought there was a lot to be learnt from such communities. They had taught me a lot.

I had been resting for a total of five weeks. I had tried to keep busy to oppose the obvious frustration of not training. I had played my berimbau to my fingers' exhaustion, watched rodas and lessons, and spoken to many Senzala Masters. I had also traveled to see the famous Iguazu falls on the border with Argentina, as well as taken three good friends from England to see some of Rio's beaches.

However, my desire to play Capoeira was becoming too great, and though I knew the hip wasn't better, it had been rested and so I came back to training. I knew I couldn't go all hands on deck as before, but wanted to see what I could do. I was lucky in Marcus and his soon-to-be wife Kristen had just arrived from England. Marcus was a Brazilian and Kristen Canadian, but they had met in England and were now in Rio for some weeks training before getting married in Marcus's home city of Curitiba, in the south of Brazil.

I was grateful for some new players. Marcus had reached a grey cord, and had been teaching the group back in England. He had had problems with his knee and was also taking his training with ease, and so we formed a good partnership. He was also very good to play Capoeira with. I had always been aiming throughout my training to develop my Capoeira as a game. I wanted to be able to do my movements with my opponent, whilst always allowing room for a threatening movement.

This was harder to do than it sounds, as it requires resisting the temptation to just try and catch your opponent, or kick him. It requires a far cleverer, more balanced approach, and also is linked to personality. I was beginning to realise that the more aggressive characters in Capoeira never fully extracted everything they could from the game. Their obsession with 'winning' meant they lost the enjoyment that is created by making a cat and mouse-like game, with each player entering and exiting each other's movements.

Marcus had a nice game that moulded nicely with my own. The Rastera or the entrance for a throw was never far from our minds, but not enough to stop the flow of the game, and I was to enjoy our games as much as any other I had had in Brazil.

Whilst I returned to my training, I began to notice large improvements in my game. It seemed that the rest had allowed my body to take in much of what it had learned in the previous months. My ginga was more balanced, my kicks straighter and, maybe through my concentration on music, I had slightly more rhythm in my game.

I still hadn't forgotten Gato's advice about using more Rasteras in my game and with this in mind, I approached my final rodas in Brazil. He asked me to try a Rastera in each game I played and so it was in my mind when I went to Toni's next class. As he often did, Toni tried to break the mould of a usual lesson of sequences, and had the class in a circle kicking in different ways with a partner, before the regular barrage of sit-ups.

The berimbau was then picked up and the games began. I bought Doburu's game and though I didn't manage a Rastera, I played as well as I had done in all my time training.

I felt the rhythm of the berimbau, stayed calm and tried to let my movements flow as much as possible. I left the lesson with the biggest smile that I had had for many weeks.

The next night I was to return to Peixinho's lesson. With my extra time with him in the house, I was feeling more comfortable talking with Peixinho, and he was very welcoming in my return to training. The lesson saw even more professors than normal, and so I felt this was a great chance to test my growing confidence.

The roda's energy was soon at a fever point and Eric had bought my game early as he often did. I managed to avoid all of his many charges at my body. After a short rest, I queued once more to enter the roda. I was soon at the front and Peixinho gave me a nod to buy the next game. I bought the game of a student of Ramos. She was a green cord who I had seen many times at training, but as with many other students, I didn't know her personally.

She played a quick game, often feinting one way, then the other, and then using a strong spinning kick to catch her opponent. I had Gato's words once more ringing through my head and as she threw one of her kicks I dropped quickly and pulled her leg with my foot. She stumbled and I saw a look of shock on her face. Gringo yellow cords weren't supposed to sweep green cords, and although she hadn't fallen, we both knew that I had caught her fair and square. My inner joy was soon being quashed however, with a desperate need to avoid a barrage of kicks. Each was a Martello and she was directing them towards my ribs and head with great speed. With distinct awkwardness and lack of style, I avoided the kicks before she offered me her hand.

The nod she gave as we ended the game was one of respect, and one I wouldn't forget for a long time. I had just achieved something I thought would never be possible when I had arrived in Brazil, caught out a green cord. It didn't make me a better player than her, but proved to me that my training and hard work was paying dividends and would do in the future. I had taken many more sweeps than I had given in the previous twelve months, but this one gave a little Capoeirista a lot of pleasure.

With the Brazilian currency continuing to head downwards, my ideas of working in Brazil had come to an end. Taking some time from training Capoeira and fixing my body was crucial if I was to continue training in the long term, and so with this in mind I decided it was best to leave for England. Tom was first however, and like with Jim, we promised to keep in contact and play in England once more.

He had had an eventful five months and trained particularly hard in the final two. Like everyone who had come to train, he had improved significantly and was sad to leave. I helped him take his bags up the steps of doom and into the awaiting taxi. I returned to the house where Mario was in his usual place in front of the house. I could see he was sad to be losing his housemates but at least he had Peixinho to look in on him on a regular basis.

The next day he was in his Salvador T shirt as I began to prepare my bags for my own exit. I had certainly accumulated many things over the year. The berimbaus were the obvious addition, but the kabasas were more awkward. This was the gourd of the berimbau, which was hollowed out by the maker. However, this made them prone to breakages and thus I had seven to take with my hand luggage. Along with my other bags, I was hoping the Italian airline I traveled on would be a little lenient.

I had a busy last two days to look forward to. As had typified much of the year, I knew I would have no time for the beach and had thus done my last walk down Ipanema the week before. Firstly was Gato's lesson, where he thanked me in front of the class for my hard work before the roda started. It was slightly ironic that his lesson had been full of gringos for my whole time until my final lesson when I was all alone with Freitas, Dolfino and the rest. Dolfino shook my hand even more fiercely than he had ever managed before and I was becoming slightly worried for its health before Gabriel saved me.

The next day saw my final full day in Rio and I met with Marcus once more for some Capoeira talk over breakfast.

I was beginning to face what I would miss when I returned to England. Being a lonesome Capoeirista in my English town meant that Capoeira conversations would be few and far between. Though it undoubtedly seemed tedious to non-Capoeiristas, I had spoken of little else over the year and this difference I knew I would feel.

I would certainly miss the breakfast too. My morning mix of bananas, yoghurt, raisins and wheat would be too time consuming for an English banker to make each day, and the thought of the two minute cereal as the grey clouds came to light wasn't over appealing. It would be hard to find a larger change. The City Favella house surrounded by friendly neighbours and gunman was an oxymoron in itself, and now I was heading back to the middle England greenery and sleepy towns. The days of risking life and limb on Rio's buses to arrive at my daily training schedule were about to be replaced with a long train commute to sit at a London desk. The warmth to the cold. The friendliness and openness to the introvert. The guns to the mobile phones.

The list was endless but I had heard too many good things of Capoeira in the UK to dismiss the near future. The sheer number of people who had come to train over the year showed the enthusiasm people had, and good teachers had arrived there to guide it. Pedro was in Scotland, my group had been growing in Cambridge and from Mestre Suassuna's group, Contra-Mestre Ponciano was now an established teacher in London. This side excited me, and gave me more than just hope that the extremes could be bridged.

What excited me more however, were my final lessons. I had decided to risk the hip and train both Peixinho's class and then Toni's afterwards. Peixinho gave his normal difficult sequences, but the fact I could do them so quickly showed how I had improved. I played as much as possible in the roda and then thanked him after. His dedication and ability had proved an inspiration and he had been an excellent teacher for me and, not to forget, a good landlord too.

I also said a goodbye to some of his students. Cutia and Dollar both wished me luck, and the quick talking Azeite, who I finally understood, gave me his usual embrace. Some of Toni's students then started arriving for his class. I would miss them even more. Samurai and his sister Geisha had always been friendly to me, and the group had its own special energy.

Toni gave his usual energetic class and ended with the endless sit-ups that he loved to lead. Everyone would have to count to ten in sequence, with some repeating. The roda then started and I managed what would be my final games in Brazil. For them to be accompanied by Toni's voice was highly pleasing. At the end I presented him with a whisky I knew would be well received and thanked him. His attitude and energy showed how much one person can add to a roda and inspire those around them. His students respect was obvious and well deserved. I also went out my way to thank

Lobo, who in Toni's absence had shown me many movements I had rarely seen in Senzala, even if I struggled with most of them.

My mind was filled with thoughts as I took the bus home for the last time. Each district I passed was filled with such distinct character. Botofogo with its arch and view of Sugar Loaf, Flamengo with its green park dividing the busy roads and then into Lapa with its nightlife and seedier side. As my bus climbed into the hills of Santa Teresa, I passed my favourite restaurants and the bars that were becoming busy with late night drinkers. It would be impossible to forget.

I was staying at Gato's house for my final night and was beginning to drift away when Gabriel arrived home from a late night guitar session. We had something to finish and so at 1am we made our way to the poolside for the final winner takes all (well just honour) game. It was to be a classic. Gabriel took a swift 2-0 lead, and it looked as if his form of the previous weeks would continue. However, my star striker was to have other ideas.

He scored two quick goals before Gabriel made it 4-2. It was first to five and I became worried. My sleepy mind had long since gone, and as Zekita the dog came to watch the excitement, a few shots ran out from the nearby Favella. I was glad I wasn't in my usual bed.

The game continued and with a free kick and a long ranger, I brought it back to 4-4. All the childish arguments from the previous months of playing would come down to one goal.

A foul gave Gabriel a good chance, but the 2-inch block that was my goalkeeper proved too much for him to beat. The ensuing counter-attack gave me my chance. Every other gringo who had visited in my time had found Gabriel's and my delicate touch of buttons either childish, ridiculous or both. However, it proved its worth as with two perfect passes, I maneuvered the small square 'ball' to my Botofogo coloured button. Gabriel moved his keeper ready for the coming shot, but nothing would stop it as it flew into the top corner of the goal.

The joy was uncontrollable as I fell to my knees laughing at the slightly lost Gabriel. His pride had been hurt as I had the final laugh. We shook hands and started laughing together, as Zekita started running around the pool, as she loved to do. Another shot in the night caused us to hurry on indoors.

As with most mornings in Brazil, there was always time for a little training, even if I did have a long haul flight to catch. Gato came up as I finished my session 'playing' and maneuvering around my favourite chair. I showed him a move I had been practicing since the Capoeirando five months previously. I never quite forgot Suassuna's lesson I never did, and showed Gato my bridge and how I too could now roll out of it too. Not quite like Suassuna's students, or Lobo had shown, but it was a start and showed how far a bit of dedication can go, and more of where it can take you.

I saw Gato smile as he asked me to try it after a kick, which I managed. The endless need for a Capoeirista to please his watching Mestre was coming to the fore once more. As I saw Gato's smile, I came over in contemplative mood. I certainly hadn't conquered Capoeira, as no one would ever do, but I had kept an open mind and tried to take every opportunity to learn as much as I could. My technique had improved, but more importantly, I had learnt that Capoeira is not a small journey of a matter of months. It is something that challenges an individual in so many different ways, and constantly offers new situations every day for a lifetime, and the roda was the preparation to face these.

I took my last freezing shower and called for a taxi. There were tears on both sides as I left Beatrice a card of thanks and shook Gato's hand. Rio's sun was beating down as we passed the Favellas onto the main motorway to the airport. I looked at my clothes and luggage. One suitcase, 7 berimbaus, 7 kebasas, one T-shirt, a pair of flip-flops and some Capoeira trousers. I was leaving Brazil, but Brazil wasn't going to be leaving me.

Glossary

Angola	the older form of Capoeira, as taught by Mestre Pastinha among others
Apelido	a nickname
Armada	an upright spinning kick
Atabaque	drum used in Capoeira
Bencao	a push kick
Berimbau	one stringed instrument used to direct the roda
Futebol de Botao	button football. Game played by pushing buttons over a playing surface

Martello	the traditional martial arts kick, done with the front of the foot, usually to the ribs or head
Meu Lua de Compasso held low	a spinning kick with the body
Meu Lua de Frente	an inward crescent kick
Pandeiro	tambourine
Queixada	an outward crescent kick
Rabo de Arraia	a movement in Angola where the body is held low as a spinning kick is given
Regional	Capoeira rhythm and style of game created by Mestre Bimba
Roda Capoeira	the circle formed to play

Tesoura	a throw where the legs are wrapped around an opponent and the body twists to make him fall
Toque	a rhythm played on the berimbau
Vigitiva	a powerful throwing movement

930126

Printed in Great Britain by
Amazon.co.uk, Ltd.,
Marston Gate.